Adventist Authority Wars, Ordination, and the Roman Catholic Temptation

Adventist Authority Wars, Ordination, and the Roman Catholic Temptation

George R. Knight

Oak and Acorn Publishing
Westlake Village, California

OAK & ACORN
PUBLISHING

For information contact:
Oak and Acorn Publishing
PO Box 5005
Westlake Village, CA   91359-5005

Cover image:
Study of a Fire at the Grand Storehouse of the Tower of London
by JMW Turner

First Edition: August 2017

10 9 8 7 6 5 4 3 2 1

"In a land of boasted freedom of thought and of conscience, like ours, church force cannot produce unity; but has caused divisions, and has given rise to religious sects and parties almost innumerable."
—James White, *Signs of the Times*, June 4, 1874

"Diversity is today a fact. The church can not repress it. It would do better to celebrate it....Unity is dependent on the recognition of diversity."
—Barry D. Oliver, *SDA Organizational Structure*, p. 346

"In no conference should propositions be rushed through without time being taken by the brethren to weigh carefully all sides of the question. ... Very many matters have been taken up and carried by vote, that have involved far more than was anticipated and far more than those who voted would have been willing to assent to had they taken time to consider the question from all sides."
—Ellen G. White, *Testimonies*, vol. 9, p. 278

"The very beginning of the great apostasy was in seeking to supplement the authority of God by that of the church."
—Ellen G. White, *The Great Controversy*, pp. 289-290

"God has not put any kingly power in our ranks to control this or that branch of the work. The work has been greatly restricted by the efforts to control it in every line.... If the work had not been so restricted by an impediment here, and an impediment there, and on the other side an impediment, it would have gone forth in its majesty."
—Ellen G. White, *General Conference Bulletin*, 1901, p. 26

"It has been a necessity to organize Union Conferences, that the General Conference shall not exercise dictation over all the separate Conferences."
—Ellen G. White, MS 26, April 3, 1903

"The real issue facing the church today is not that of the ordination of women, but the proper use of authority."
—George R. Knight

Contents

You Must Read This First:
It Sets the Stage

I am becoming an old man, and up until recently my great desire has been to avoid controversy and die in peace. But of late that wish has become to die in one piece. I have failed in the first of those goals, but still hope to succeed in the second.

The occasion for this book began harmlessly enough. In late June 2015 the lead pastor of my local congregation in Medford, Oregon, asked me to preach a sermon on the biblical meaning of ordination. It seemed to be an appropriate topic since the 2015 General Conference session would convene a few days later in San Antonio, Texas, and the most anticipated event at that convention would be the vote regarding whether each of the world divisions would have the option of ordaining female pastors.

Interestingly, up to that time I had never spoken or written on the topic of ordination. Believing that there were many people more qualified than me to handle the subject, I had been neglecting it. I was 10 years into my retirement and had no desire for controversy.

The topic of ordination had never been of special interest in Adventism before the 1960s and 1970s. In fact, the denomination was in the habit of ordaining non-pastor conference treasurers, college presidents, and other non-pastoral functionaries on a regular basis, perhaps to allow them to be remunerated at a better rate. But that lack of interest would take a radical turn when the rising number of female pastors and chaplains began to think in terms of ordination. And that interest eventually turned into controversy.

The background to the present book became more intense in the 1990s when the 1990 and 1995 General Conference sessions took actions on the appropriateness of world divisions having the option of ordaining female pastors if they so desired. The vote in both cases was negative. Female pastors could be "commissioned" ministers but not "ordained." The struggle between those in favor of female ordination and those opposed formed along different hermeneutical perspectives. That is, the two opposing positions lined up along two different approaches to the interpretation of the Bible. Thus hermeneutics became central to the entire debate.

Some felt the issue had forever been solved in 1995. But it was not to be. As the number of truly successful female pastors continued to grow so did the discussion of their possible ordination. The intensity of the discussion continued to build in the early years of the 21st century. By the time of the 2010 General Conference session it was realized that the topic was not going to go away. As a result, in 2011 the General Conference leadership established the Theology of Ordination Study Committee (TOSC) to study the topic thoroughly and to develop a consensus statement on the theology of ordination and on the propriety of ordaining women for those divisions that wished to do so. Consensus was achieved on the first of those goals, but the second generated vigorous dissension between those for and those opposed to the ordination of female pastors. But the final vote in June 14, 2014, was clear. A super majority of 62 to 32 recommended that each of the denomination's world divisions should have the option of ordaining women to the pastoral ministry if so desired.

The unfortunate aftermath of the TOSC decision is that the vote in favor of giving divisions a choice on the ordination issue was not reported to the voting delegates at the General Conference session in 2015. Nor was the fact that nearly all of the world divisions in their individual TOSC reports favored each division having a choice. That is an almost unbelievable neglect, given the fact that the denomination had spent hundreds of thousands of dollars on the TOSC project to solve the problem once and for all. Why the findings were not reported has never been publicly explained. So we are left to speculate that perhaps the committee did not come up with the "proper" conclusions. The long-awaited vote in 2015 found a deeply divided denomination, with 58% voting against the choice-by-division option and 42% voting for it.

The 2015 vote, as might be expected, left those union conferences that were already ordaining female pastors (on the basis of the *General Conference Working Policy's* stipulation that it was union conferences that were to decide who would be ordained) in a difficult spot. Because of the uncomfortableness of its position, the Columbia Union Conference in the North American Division held a Leadership Summit on Mission and Governance in March 2016. That meeting left no doubt on its continuing determination to ordain female pastors.

That determination and other practices, such as abolishing the category of "ordination" and commissioning both males and females in the Norwegian Union of Churches, led certain administrators in the General Conference to initiate punitive procedures against those unions in "rebellion." The most radical of those measures came out of the presidential offices in September 2016 in anticipation of the Annual Council of the General Conference Executive Committee, which would meet the next month. In essence, the presidential suggestion was to dissolve the noncompliant unions (in this case the Columbia and Pacific Union Conferences), recreate them as union missions, appoint more compliant leaders, and hopefully get the constituents to change their vote on the ordination of females.

That proposal apparently was deemed to be a bit hasty. As a result, the General Conference Secretariat set forth a more moderate approach in a 50-page document titled "A Study of Church Governance and Unity," which definitely set forth authority in Seventh-day Adventism as flowing down from the General Conference to the constituent administrative entities of the denomination. That position was quite at variance with the traditional position of Adventism in which authority was located in the constituents and flowed upward. The eventual outcome of the 2016 Annual Council was a decision to create a procedure to discipline those unions out of harmony with the General Conference on the topic of the ordination of female pastors. That move seems to be understandable. But what is not so easy to understand is why a new procedure was deemed necessary, since such a policy was already firmly in place in the *Working Policy*. The difficulty appears to be that, according to existing policy, all such punitive actions are to begin at the level of the divisions. In this case, some must have feared that the North American Division would not come up with the "appropriate" solution. So we find the General Conference leadership in the interesting situation of stepping outside of a voted policy to punish those unions it deemed to be outside of voted policy.

That brings us to June 2017 and the Unity Conference called to meet in London by 10 union conferences from four of the church's world divisions to discuss how best to relate to the situation they expected to meet at the 2017 Annual Council; namely, the procedures expected to be put in place to bring those unions in "rebellion" into line. The meeting was called for openly, and all administrators, scholars, and other leaders were invited to attend. The General Conference president was invited to make a presentation. He declined, but did go on record that the meeting was an "unauthorized" meeting and that General Conference travel budgets could not be used to finance attendance. More to the point was the use of financial and other pressure to assure that the meetings were not supported. Thus the London meetings found no participants from Andrews University's theological seminary or other General Conference institutions. The same can be said for certain other institutions of higher learning around the world. Also, current administrators who valued their future got the avoidance message. But in spite of the implied and explicit threats, the London meetings witnessed a strong attendance. The atmosphere was one of dedication in support of the denomination's principles and goals.

While writing this preface I received an announcement of a forthcoming convention to be held in August 2017 on the same topic as the London meeting. Its official title is "Scripture, Church Structure, and the Path to Unity Symposium." The participants in the forthcoming symposium are well known to represent the core of those who stand against the position taken by the Pacific, Columbia, and other "noncompliant" unions. But what is most interesting is that one of the presenters is a current General Conference vice president. Thus, one of my friends has pointed out, "either these are 'official church meetings,'" or the General Conference president "has had a change of heart," or "we have a double standard going on here." (Since writing the above, the General Conference dignitary is no longer being advertised as a featured speaker. I do not know the reason for the change, but one speculative possibility is that someone may have pointed out the double standard. Of course, there are better reasons, such as these meetings are also "not authorized." But as yet I have seen no announcement to that effect.)

The good news about the symposium is that its promoters have put their finger on the real issue. Their advertising notes that the symposium is not about women's ordination but church authority and the basis for unity. And on that both perspectives appear to agree. The real issue in Adventism today is not the ordination of female pastors but the issue of authority. In that it finds a parallel in the 16th-century Protestant Reformation, a movement that at its core was not about indulgences or justification by faith but about ecclesiastical authority. In the present situation the ordination of women is merely the topic that has given rise to the struggle over authority.

With that fact in mind I have organized the present book with issues in authority forming Part I and issues related to ordination and hermeneutics forming Part II. While in current history the two issues have become intertwined, we always need to keep in mind that the topic of authority is basic while that of ordination is merely the stimulus that brought the authoritative crisis point to the surface.

And we should note that the current situation is not the first "authority war" in the denomination. One only has to think of the ongoing conflict in the 1850s between the various sectors of Adventism to even establish a formal church organization. Just as serious and just as brutal was the 1888 conflict over the law in Galatians and the 10 horns of Daniel 7. Authority wars have been periodic in Seventh-day Adventist history. And, interestingly enough, in the two illustrations above, both wars were fought on the basis of two varying sets of hermeneutical principles. The same can be said of the long battle over the daily in the 1910s, the king of the north a decade later, and the denomination's understanding of Ellen White later in the century. Struggles over theology, hermeneutics, and church authority go hand in hand throughout the denomination's history. Before moving away from the topic of authority wars, I should point out that the struggle during the 1888 period and the current situation exhibit a great many parallels, including those of the spirit and the divisiveness of some of the participants.

In terms of the current book, my June 2015 ordination sermon, which immediately had gone viral on the Internet, led to the invitation by the Columbia Union to present two papers at its Leadership Summit in March 2016. Those two papers—"The Anti-organizational People Organize in Spite of Themselves" and "The Role of Union Conferences in Relation to Higher Authorities"—form the first two chapters. My participation in that meeting resulted in an invitation to present a paper at the Unity meetings in London in June 2017. That paper, "Catholic or Adventist: The Ongoing Struggle Over Authority + 9.5 Theses," is the third chapter.

With Chapters 4-6 we come to a major shift in subject matter. Here we move away from the primary topic of church authority to the secondary issue of female ordination and hermeneutical issues related to the discussion. Chapter 4, "The Biblical Meaning of Ordination," is the transcription of the June 2015 sermon that spurred the chain of events that led up to the publication of this book. Chapter 5, "Proving More Than Intended," was first published in *Ministry* in March 1996. It was stimulated by my reaction to the major formal presentation at the 1995 General Conference session in opposition to the ordination of female pastors. Given the methodology and passages used, my conclusion was that what the speaker had really demonstrated was that Ellen White was a false prophet, which certainly was not the presenter's intention. Chapter 6, "Ecclesiastical Deadlock: James White Solves a Problem That Had No Answer," was initially developed for the 2015 book entitled *Women and Ordination: Biblical and Historical Studies*. The chapter develops the radical hermeneutical transformation that allowed the denomination to organize in a manner that is not specifically authorized in the Bible. Women's ordination is then viewed from that hermeneutical perspective.

Here I need to indicate that I have opted to present this book as individual essays in the flow of history rather than to meld them into a format of continuous flow as I would have done if I had chosen to refine the essays into what we typically think of as a "book" rather than a collection of papers. As a result, I HAVE CHOSEN NOT TO REMOVE THE REDUNDANCIES IN THE TEXT. In other words, I want the reader to have the full content of each paper as it was presented in its historical context. Thus the argument developed in each document stands as it was originally developed without having to refer to other chapters. The positive aspect of that approach is that each document retains its original unity and flow. The negative side is that there is some redundancy. However, the positive aspect of the negative side is that repetition is a law of learning and those things that are repeated are generally worth remembering. The one exception to my non-removal policy is in Chapter 6, in which I removed a large redundant section that was not needed to make the forceful point of the paper.

One of the more interesting events following my presentation of "Catholic or Adventist: The Ongoing Struggle Over Authority + 9.5

Theses" has been the banning of the sale of my books in the Michigan Conference's bookstores. The ban was reversed, but correspondents from around the world consistently have noted two points: first, that the action would undoubtedly boost the sale of my books; second, that the action merely reinforced my point that administrative Adventism in its authoritative approach all too often takes the path of the medieval church. After all, the medieval church regularly banned books it didn't like through its Index of forbidden books. In the long run, the most significant result of the ban will be increased readers for the present volume. It is what I like to think of as "the book that should have been banned." There is no way I could have paid for the vast amount of advertising I received through worldwide Internet discussion of the ban. (Since the above was written, the Michigan Conference president has reinstated the ban on my books. His latest decision is that the stores may sell existing stock, but are not to place any orders to replenish their stock when it runs out.)

In the dialogue that followed the ban, the opinion was expressed that the books of anyone who challenges the General Conference president's authority should not be on the shelves of Adventist Book Centers. One perceptive respondent noted that if that were the case they would have to remove Ellen G. White's books also.

Meanwhile, I need to express my love and concern for my church and its leaders, even those who disagree with me. And I want to say that my personal dealings with the current General Conference president have been consistently pleasant. I know him to be a man of prayer, a Christian gentleman, and a person who fervently believes in the mission of the Seventh-day Adventist Church. Where we differ is on administrative style. On that topic I have said some straightforward things in this book. While I firmly hold to what I have said, I would hope and pray that God would give me the grace to change if it is demonstrated that I am in the wrong. I can only hope and pray for the same for those who disagree with me and for those who have been on the receiving end of some of my sentences. If I have erred, I hope for their forgiveness. But if I am correct, I would love to see change. I have given my life to supporting the Seventh-day Adventist Church. I love my church and only want the best for it and its leaders. And "best" always means being faithful to the Bible, the prophetic gift of Ellen White, and the great principles demonstrated in Adventist history. My prayer for each reader is that he or she will read with both eyes open and let the Spirit guide.

George R. Knight
Rogue River, Oregon
July 30, 2017

Part I

Adventist Authority Wars
and the
Roman Catholic Temptation

CHAPTER ONE

The Anti-organizational People Organize in Spite of Themselves[1*]

Anti-organizational in the extreme is the only proper description for those independent Bible students who would form the Seventh-day Adventist Church in the 1860s, nearly 20 years after the end of Millerism. Their antipathy towards organized churches finds its roots in the period before the 1844 Disappointment.

An Anti-organizational Heritage

Pre-disappointment attitudes toward organization followed two lines. The first is the organizational position of the Christian Connexion to which two (James White and Joseph Bates) of the three founders of Seventh-day Adventism belonged. According to an 1836 history, the movement arose in several parts of the United States in

---

* The present chapter was developed as a presentation for the "Leadership Summit on Mission and Governance" sponsored by the Columbia Union Conference in March 2016. The stimulus for the meetings was the fact that the Columbia Union Conference had been ordaining women to ministry and was therefore out of harmony with the General Conference as expressed in the 2015 session vote.

the early 1800s "not so much to establish any peculiar and distinctive doctrines, as *to assert, for individuals and churches, more liberty and independence* in relation to matters of faith and practice, to *shake off the authority* of human creeds and the shackles of prescribed modes and forms, to make the Bible their only guide, claiming for every man the right to be his own expositor of it, to judge, for himself, what are its doctrines and requirements, and in practice, to follow more strictly the simplicity of the apostles and primitive Christians." The movement *opposed any "infringement of Christian liberty,"* in terms of both creedal statements and structural governance.[2]

In spite of their radical independence, the Connexionists did grant the need for structure at the local church level, but they considered "each church" or congregation "an independent body, possessing exclusive authority to regulate and govern its own affairs."[3] The movement was held together by periodicals and periodic meetings or conferences.

The second line of development in Adventism's anti-organizational stance is the Millerite experience. Unlike the Connexionists, most Millerite Adventists were not anti-organizational in their attitudes during the early years of their movement. On the other hand, they had no desire to form their own organization. To the contrary, they sought to remain in the various denominations while they witnessed to their Advent faith and waited for Christ's coming. Time was too short for any new organization.

The fact that the Millerites did not have a separate denominational organization did not mean that they lacked structure. Joshua V. Himes had welded them into an impressive missionary movement that reflected his Connexionist background. As a result, we find periodicals and regular general conference meetings at the heart of the forward drive of Millerism. Those two elements formed the "structure" of the Millerite Adventist movement.

That "structure" constituted one aspect of Millerism's contribution to early Sabbatarian Adventism's attitude toward church organization. The second aspect had to do with the conflict between Millerism and the denominations. It was one thing to agitate for the Advent message from within the denominations when the event was a few years off. But it was quite another thing as the year of the end approached. Increasing conflict arose as Millerite ministers lost their pulpits and Miller's followers were excluded from fellowship.

It is in that context that Charles Fitch in July 1843 published what became one of the most influential Millerite sermons. Based on Revelation 14:8 and 18:1-5, it was titled "'Come Out of Her My People.'" In essence, those apocalyptic passages deal with both the fall of Babylon and the consequent need of God's people to flee from the corrupt system it represented. For Fitch, Babylon included all those who rejected the message of Christ's soon coming.[4]

One Millerite preacher who felt especially impressed to proclaim the message to leave other churches was George Storrs. Storrs wrote that Babylon "is the *old mother* and all her children [the Protestant denominations]; who are known by the family likeness, a domineering, lordly spirit; a spirit to suppress a free search after truth, and a free expression of our conviction of what is truth."[5]

Individuals needed to abandon the denominations because "we have no right to let any men, or body of men, thus lord it over us. And to remain in such an organized body...is to remain in Babylon." To Storrs the history of organized religion (both Catholic and Protestant) was one of bigotry and persecution. He argued against visible, organized churches and opted for God's great invisible church that "the Lord organizes" on the basis of the "bonds of love." In the face of persecution caused by a sincere belief in the soon coming of Jesus, Storrs concluded that "no church can be organized by man's invention but what it becomes Babylon *the moment it is organized.*"[6]

One Millerite family that experienced the persecuting force of the denominations was that of young Ellen Harmon, which was disfellowshipped from the Methodist Episcopal Church of Portland, Maine, in September 1843.[7] Through that experience Ellen had witnessed firsthand the unjustness of a highly centralized denomination that in the state of Maine had systematically purged both laypeople and ministers who would not renounce their Millerite beliefs.

While not all Millerites accepted Storrs' extreme conclusions, his message, along with the believers' painful experiences at the hands of organized churches, left an indelible impression on the great bulk of the believers. It was so strong that all Millerite groups found it next to impossible to organize to any significant extent after the Great Disappointment of October 22, 1844.

Early Sabbatarian Adventist Moves
Toward Organization, 1844-1854

As noted above, all three of the founders of Seventh-day Adventism had reasons to fear organized religion. Beyond that, they also belonged to that sector of post-disappointment Adventism that believed that the door of probation had closed and that their mission to the world at large had been completed in 1844. Because of that belief they felt no desire to organize for reasons of evangelism or mission.

The first stimulus to change was the felt need to share the theological insights they had gained between 1845 and 1847 with other shut-door Adventists. At this early date, however, they felt no need to share their understanding of the Bible with the larger world since they had not yet worked through their erroneous idea that probation had already closed.

They viewed their rather limited mission to ex-Millerites in terms of what they labeled the scattering and gathering times. The scattering time had begun in late October 1844 with the splintering of the Millerite movement. But by 1848 the Whites and Bates were absolutely convinced that they had the answer for the scattered believers. James White put it nicely in November 1849: "The scattering time we have had; it is in the past, and now the time for the saints to be gathered into the unity of the faith, and be sealed by one holy, uniting truth *has come*. Yes, Brother, *it has come*."[8]

Sabbatarian outreach during the gathering time took two forms. One consisted of periodic conferences to help bring about unity of belief. The first of the Sabbatarian conferences convened in the spring of 1848. The main purpose of the conferences was evangelistic, to unite a body of believers on the three angels' messages.[9]

The second avenue that the Sabbatarian leadership used to gather in a people involved the development of various periodicals. At the Sabbatarian conference held in Dorchester, Massachusetts, during November 1848, Ellen White had a vision with special implications for her husband. After coming out of it, she told him that he "must begin to print a little paper and send it out to the people." It would be small at first, but eventually it would be "like streams of light that went clear round the world."[10] In response to that vision, James White began publishing *Present Truth* in July 1849, a periodical that evolved into *The Second Advent Review and Sabbath Herald* by November 1850.

We should note that the two methods that the Sabbatarians used to gather in a people were not only evangelistic but also provided *their first organizational format.* The 1850s would witness the continuation of periodic conferences as the various congregations of Sabbathkeeping Adventists sent members to represent them in general meetings of Sabbatarian believers.

The *Review and Herald* not only printed notices and resolutions of those meetings but also provided the scattered Sabbatarians with news of their "church" and fellow believers, sermons, and a sense of belonging. Thus the *Review* was probably the most effective instrument in both gathering and uniting the body of believers.

Throughout the 1850s the Sabbatarian movement would consist of a loose association of congregations and individuals united through the agency of periodicals and "conferences," or general meetings, of believers. Thus, whether they realized it or not, *the Sabbatarians were operating with the same type of church order as that of the Connexionists and the Millerites.* But the continuation of time, the rapid growth in the number of Sabbatarians, and their expanding vision of mission would soon demand further organizational initiatives.

Another stimulus that drove the Sabbatarians toward developing a more extensive system of church organization derived from a need to maintain ethical and doctrinal unity. Problems related to those issues would arise soon after the beginning of the gathering time and would culminate in both of the Whites firmly appealing for "gospel order" in the latter part of 1853.

But even before that date the Whites had indicated the need for order to save the movement from such things as fanaticism and false preachers. Ellen White, for example, called the Sabbatarians to move according to "Bible order" in 1850.[11]

The rapid growth of the Sabbatarian movement also necessitated some sort of order or structure. By 1852 there may have been as many as 2,000 Sabbatarian Adventists. While that growth was good, it brought with it new problems and challenges while aggravating some of the older problems already facing the young movement. Many new congregations of Sabbathkeepers had formed, but no order existed among them even at the congregational level. That made them easy prey to fanatics and unauthorized preachers from both inside and outside their local group. Such a state of affairs in 1851 led the Whites to believe that the movement required their personal presence from time to time to modify and correct abuses. Thus the next few years would see their reports in the *Review* with such titles as "Our Tour East."

On those tours the Whites dealt with such issues as fanaticism, disfellowshipping, and the "importance of union." We also find in 1851 the first information we have on the appointment of local church officers.[12] That same year the *Review* also reported the first ordination in Adventist records. Washington Morse was apparently ordained to the gospel ministry.[13]

By 1852 the Sabbatarians had come to see themselves less as a "scattered flock" and more as a church. A reinterpretation of the shut-door doctrine accompanied that recognition. They gradually concluded that probation for the world at large had not closed in 1844 and that they had a mission to those who had not been in the Millerite movement. Such realizations would add their weight in pressing the Sabbatarians toward a more substantial organization.

The major problem they faced in the early 1850s was that they had no systematic defense against impostors. Almost anybody who wanted to could preach in Sabbatarian congregations. Large sectors of Adventism had no checks on ministerial orthodoxy or even morality as it faced the crisis of a self-appointed ministry.

The year 1853 would see the Sabbatarians take two steps to protect their congregations from "false" brethren. First, the leading Sabbatarian ministers adopted a plan whereby approved preachers received a card "recommending them to the fellowship of the Lord's people everywhere, simply stating that they were approved in the work of the gospel ministry." Two ministers known by Sabbatarian Adventists to be leaders of the movement dated and signed the cards.[14]

The second method utilized by the Sabbatarians to certify their leaders was ordination. By late 1853 they regularly ordained both traveling preachers (ministers assigned to specific congregations did not yet exist) and deacons (who appear to be the only local church officers at that early period).

But even those actions had not solved the problem. As a result, both James and Ellen White issued major calls for "gospel order" in December 1853. James led the assault for better organization with four articles in the *Review* entitled "Gospel Order." His December 6 article redefined Babylon in the Sabbatarian context. "It is a lamentable fact," he asserted, "that many of our Advent brethren who made a timely escape from the bondage of the different churches [Babylon]...have since *been in a more perfect Babylon than ever before. Gospel order has been too much overlooked by them.... Many in their zeal to come out of Babylon, partook of a rash, disorderly spirit, and were soon found in a perfect Babel of confusion.... To suppose that the church of Christ is free from restraint and discipline, is the wildest fanaticism.*"[15]

Late December 1853 also saw Ellen White's first extensive call for further order. Basing her sentiments on a vision received during her and James' eastern tour in the fall of 1852, she wrote that "*the Lord has shown that gospel order has been too much feared and neglected.*

Formality should be shunned; but, in so doing, order should not be neglected. There is order in heaven. There was order in the church when Christ was upon the earth, and after His departure order was strictly observed among His apostles. And now *in these last days*, while God is bringing His children into the unity of the faith, *there is more real need of order than ever before.*" Most of her article dealt with the problems raised by the "self-sent messengers" who were "a curse to the cause" of the Sabbatarians. As did James, she dealt with the qualifications of ministers and the ordination of those approved by "brethren of experience and of sound minds."[16]

By the beginning of 1854 James and Ellen White were quite settled on the need for more order and structure among the Sabbatarians. James not only considered it important, he also believed that the movement wouldn't see much growth without it.[17]

The fact that Sabbatarian Adventism also faced its first organized schisms at that time, beginning with the Messenger Party in 1854, undoubtedly reinforced James' convictions on the topic of gospel order. With that in mind, it is little wonder that the second half of the 1850s saw an increasing number of articles reflecting a developing understanding of Bible principles related to church order and the ordination of approved leaders.

Joseph Bates was quite convinced that biblical church order must be restored to the church before the Second Advent. He was also clear that it was the apostolic order of the church that needed to be restored. He made no room for any element of organization not found in the New Testament.[18] James White at this early period shared a similar opinion. Thus he could write in 1854 that "by gospel, or church order we mean that order in church association and discipline taught in the gospel of Jesus Christ by the writers of the New

Testament."[19] A few months later he spoke of the "perfect system of order, set forth in the New Testament, by inspiration of God.... The Scriptures present a perfect system, which, if carried out, will save the Church from imposters" and provide the ministers with an adequate platform for carrying out the work of the church.[20]

J. B. Frisbie, the most active writer in the *Review* in the mid-1850s on church order, *agreed with Bates and White that every aspect of church order needed to be explicitly spelled out in the Bible*. Thus he argued against any church name except the *one* given by God in the Bible: "The Church of God." Any other name "savors more of Babylon...than it does" of God's church. By the same logic, Frisbie implied in agreement with others that they should not keep church membership lists since the names of God's children are recorded in the books of heaven.[21]

With their literalistic biblical approach to church order it is of little surprise that Frisbie and others soon began to discuss the duty of a second local church officer—the elder. In January 1855 he noted that there were "two classes of preaching elders" in the New Testament churches—"traveling elders" and "local elders." The traveling elders had a supervisory role over several churches, whereas "local elders...had the pastoral care and oversight of one church." He went on to observe that local churches should have both elders and deacons. The first, he pointed out, "had the oversight of the spiritual, the other the temporal affairs of the church."[22] By the end of the year Sabbatarians were ordaining local elders as well as deacons and pastors.

Gradually they were strengthening gospel order at the level of the local church. In fact, the individual congregation was the only level of organization that most Sabbatarians gave much thought to. Thus such leaders as Bates could preface an extended article on "Church

Order" with the following definition: "*Church, signifies a particular congregation of believers* in Christ, united together in the order of the gospel."[23]

Moving Beyond Concerns with Local Church Organization, 1855-1859

In the second half of the 1850s the church-order debate among Sabbatarians would focus on what it meant for congregations to be "united together." At least four issues would force leaders such as James White to look at church organization more globally. The first had to do with the legal ownership of property—especially the publishing office and church buildings. The responsibility of owning everything in his own name prompted White to resign as editor of the *Review* in late 1855. Not being ready yet for legal incorporation, he suggested that a committee own the publishing house and that a financial committee handle the business matters related to the Sabbatarians' growing publishing enterprise.[24] Similar suggestions appeared in regard to the holding of church property.

A second issue pushing White and others toward a broader church organization concerned the problem of paying preachers. He had first raised the topic in 1849. But talking about the issue without some sort of system to deal with it didn't help much. In fact, as the Sabbatarian work expanded, things got worse. Sabbatarian preachers were overworked and underpaid—a sure formula for disaster.

A case in point involved young John Nevins Andrews, a man who later served the church as its leading scholar, its first "official" foreign missionary, and a General Conference president. But in the mid-1850s exhaustion and deprivation had forced him into retiring from the ministry while only in his mid-20s. The fall of 1856 found him becoming a clerk in his uncle's store in Waukon, Iowa. Waukon, in fact, was rapidly becoming a colony of apathetic Sabbatarian Adventists. Another leading minister who fled to Waukon in 1856 was John N. Loughborough, who had become, as he put it, "somewhat discouraged as to finances."[25] The Whites temporarily averted a crisis in the Adventist ministry by making a danger-filled midwinter journey across the ice-clogged Mississippi River to Waukon to wake up the sleeping Adventist community and to reclaim the dropout ministers. But their rededication did not change the objective financial realities.

Anticipating the financial problems, the Battle Creek, Michigan, congregation formed a study group in the spring of 1858 to search the Bible for a plan to support the ministry. Under the leadership of Andrews, the group developed a report accepted in early 1859. The plan of Systematic Benevolence (or "Sister Betsy," as many nicknamed it) encouraged men to contribute 5 to 25 cents per week, and women 2 to 10 cents. In addition, both groups were assessed 1 to 5 cents per week for each $100 unit of property they owned.[26]

James White was jubilant over the plan, believing that it would leave the ministers free from financial embarrassment so that they could work more effectively. His wife was equally grateful. "I saw," she penned in 1859, "that there should be order in the church of God, and that system is needed in carrying forward successfully the last great message of mercy to the world. God is leading His people in the plan of systematic benevolence."[27]

Of course, it was one thing to have a plan for paying preachers and quite another thing to administrate it in a religious group that had no settled pastors. Proper collection and distribution of the funds logically predicated organizational developments beyond the congregational level.

Closely related to a system for remunerating preachers was a third issue that drove White to a broader form of church organization—the assignment of preachers. In 1859 White wrote that whereas such communities as Battle Creek often had several preachers on hand, others remained "destitute, not having heard a discourse for three months." Recognizing the situation to be a genuine problem, White went on to note that "system in labor, or, in locating preachers' families near their fields of labor, may be called for" as well as financial support. He appealed to the churches to send their requests to him personally.[28]

Thus it appears that by 1859 James White was *acting* the part of superintendent in the assignment and paying of preachers, but without any official structure to undergird his efforts. Such a situation was not only difficult; it also left him open to criticism regarding mismanagement and the misappropriation of funds. He had come to realize that Sabbatarians needed a broader system.

A fourth problem that raised the issue of a more adequate church structure resulted from the question of transferring membership. It was especially difficult when a person had been disfellowshipped by one congregation and desired fellowship with another. How should they handle membership transfers between congregations? And how should independent congregations relate to each other?[29]

By the middle of 1859 White was ready to open the final drive for formal denominational organization. At a conference of believers held in Battle Creek he presented a major paper on Systematic Benevolence, since "the shortness of time and the vast importance of the truth calls upon us in the most imperative manner to extend missionary labor."[30]

The next month he laid down the gauntlet in no uncertain terms.

"*We lack system,*" he cried on July 21. "Many of our brethren are in a scattered state. They observe the Sabbath, read with some interest the Review; but beyond this *they are doing but little or nothing for want of some method of united action among them.*" To meet the situation, he called for regular meetings in each state (yearly in some and four or five times a year in others) to give guidance to the work of the Sabbatarians in that region.[31]

"We are aware," he wrote, "that these suggestions will not meet the minds of all. Bro. Over-cautious will be frightened, and will be ready to warn his brethren to be careful and not venture out too far; while Bro. Confusion will cry out, 'O, this looks just like Babylon! Following the fallen church!' Bro. Do-little will say, 'The cause is the Lord's, and we had better leave it in his hands, he will take care of it.' 'Amen,' says Love-this-world, Slothful, Selfish, and Stingy, 'if God calls men to preach, let them go out and preach, he will take care of them, and those who believe their message;' while Korah, Dathan and Abiram are ready to rebel against those who feel the weight of the cause [e.g., James White] and who watch for souls as those who must give account, and raise the cry, 'Ye take too much upon you.'"[32]

White let it be known in the most descriptive language that he was sick and tired of the cry of Babylon every time that anyone mentioned organization. "Bro. Confusion," he penned, "makes a most egregious blunder in calling system, which is in harmony with the Bible and good sense, Babylon. *As Babylon signifies confusion, our erring brother has the very word stamped upon his own forehead. And we venture to say that there is not another people under heaven more worthy of the brand of Babylon than those professing the Advent faith who reject Bible order.* Is it not high time that we as a people heartily embrace everything that is good and right in the churches? Is it not blind folly to start back at the idea of system, found everywhere in the Bible, simply because it is observed in the fallen churches?"[33]

As one who had the "weight of the cause" upon him, James White felt impelled to take his stand for better organization among Sabbatarians. Castigating those who thought that "all that was necessary to run a train of cars was to use the brake well,"[34] he firmly believed that in order to get the Advent movement moving it had to organize. That task he would pursue with full vigor between 1860 and 1863.

Meanwhile, James' strategic place in the Sabbatarian movement had given him a scope of vision that not only separated him from the reasoning processes of many of his fellow believers but had transformed his own thinking. Three points White raised in 1859 are of special importance as we look forward to his organizing activities in the early 1860s.

First, he had moved beyond the biblical literalism of his earlier days when he believed that the Bible must explicitly spell out each aspect of church organization. In 1859 he argued that "we should not be afraid of that system which is not opposed by the Bible, and is approved by sound sense."[35] Thus he had come to a new hermeneutic. *He had moved from a principle of Bible interpretation that held that the only things Scripture allowed were those things it explicitly approved to a hermeneutic that approved of anything that did not contradict the Bible.* That shift was essential to the creative steps in church organization he would advocate in the 1860s.

That revised hermeneutic, however, put White in opposition to those, such as Frisbie and R. F. Cottrell, who maintained a literalistic approach to the Bible that demanded that it explicitly spell something out before the church could accept it. To answer that mentality, White noted that nowhere in the Bible did it say that Christians should have a weekly paper, operate a steam printing press, build places of worship, or publish books. He went on to argue that the "living church of God" needed to move forward with prayer and common sense.[36]

White's second point involves a redefinition of Babylon. The earliest Adventists had approached the concept in relation to oppression and applied it to the existing denominations. White reinterpreted it in terms of confusion and applied it to his fellow Sabbatarians. By 1859 his goal had advanced to steering the Advent cause between the twin pitfalls of Babylon as oppressor and Babylon as confusion. White's third point concerned mission. Sabbatarians must organize if they were to fulfill their responsibility to preach the three angels' messages.

Thus between 1856 and 1859 White had shifted from a literalistic perspective to one much more pragmatic. That move had not come easily. But with a sense of responsibility to face the hard facts of life he, unlike some of his colleagues, had been forced to deal pragmatically with the issues in a realistic way. He felt impelled to move on, and would in the next three years take aggressive steps to put Adventism on a firm organizational base in harmony with Bible principles and commensurate with its mission in the world.

The Final Drive for Effective Organization, 1860-1863

The final drive toward effective organization had three basic steps. The first had to do with the incorporation of church property so that it could be legally held and insured. James White raised the issue in February 1860. He flatly stated that he refused to sign notes making him personally responsible to individuals who desired to lend their money to the publishing house. Thus the movement needed to make arrangements to hold church property in a "proper manner."[37]

White's suggestion called forth a vigorous reaction from R. F. Cottrell—a corresponding editor of the *Review* and the leader of those opposed to church organization. Recognizing that a church could not incorporate unless it had a name, Cottrell wrote that he believed "it would be wrong to 'make us a name,' since that lies at the foundation of Babylon." His suggestion was that Adventists needed to trust in the Lord, who would repay them for any unjust losses at the end of time. "If any man proves a Judas, we can still bear the loss and trust the Lord."[38]

The next issue of the *Review* saw a spirited response from White, who expressed himself "not a little surprised" at Cottrell's remarks. He pointed out that the publishing office alone had thousands of dollars invested "without one legal owner." "The Devil is not dead," he asserted, and under such circumstances he knew how to shut down the publishing house.

White went on to claim that he regarded "it dangerous to leave with the Lord what he has left with us." We must operate "in a legal manner" if we are to be God's faithful stewards. That is "the only way we can handle real estate in this world."[39] He reiterated that same argument on April 26, pointing out, as he had earlier, that not every Christian duty is explicitly laid out in the Bible. At that point he wrote that "we believe it safe to be governed by the following rule. All means which, according to sound judgment, will advance the cause of truth, and are not forbidden by plain scripture declarations, should be employed."[40] With that pronouncement White placed himself fully on the platform of a pragmatic, commonsense approach to all issues not definitely settled in the Bible.

Ellen White agreed with her husband on the topic of church organization. She penned that Cottrell had taken a "wrong stand" and that "his articles were perfectly calculated to have a scattering influence, to lead minds to wrong conclusions." Then she put her influence behind that of her husband's in calling for church order so as "to place the matters of the church in a more secure position, where Satan cannot come in and take advantage."[41]

The pages of the *Review* throughout the summer of 1860 indicate that some of the Sabbatarians were coming more into harmony with James White on the topic of incorporating the publishing house and other aspects of organization. In the meantime, certain individual congregations had begun to organize legally in mid-1860 in order to protect their property.[42]

The property difficulty came to a head at a conference James White called in Battle Creek to discuss the problem along with the related issues of legal incorporation and a formal name, a requirement for incorporation. Between September 29 and October 2, 1860, delegates from at least five states discussed the situation and possible solutions in great detail. All agreed that whatever they did should be according to the Bible, but as we might expect, they disagreed over the hermeneutical issue of whether something needed to be explicitly mentioned in the Bible. James White, as usual, argued that "every Christian duty is not given in the Scriptures."[43] That essential point had to be recognized before they could make any progress toward legal organization. Gradually, as the various problems and options surfaced, the majority of the candidates accepted White's hermeneutical rule.

The October 1860 conference accomplished three main goals. The first involved the adoption of a constitution for the legal incorporation of the publishing association. The second was that "individual churches so...organize as to hold their church property or church buildings legally."[44]

The third goal accomplished at the October 1860 meetings concerned the selection of a denominational name, since the delegates finally agreed that there was no way to escape being viewed as a denomination by those looking at the movement from the outside. Many favored the name "Church of God," but the group did not accept it because several other religious bodies already used it. James White noted that the name adopted should not be objectionable to the world at large. Finally, David Hewitt resolved "that we take the name of Seventh-day Adventists." His motion carried, many delegates recognizing that it was "expressive of our faith and [doctrinal] position."[45]

The 1860 meetings had accomplished much, but much yet remained to be done. The second stage in the final drive toward effective organization had to do with the formation of local conferences in 1861. A special meeting was called to meet at Battle Creek between April 26 and 29 to discuss the issue. That meeting took two important actions. First, it took the final steps to fully legalize the publishing house. Thus the incorporation of the Seventh-day Adventist Publishing Association became official on May 3.

Of equal importance was J. N. Loughborough's call for a "more complete organization of the church." In response to that plea, the delegates voted that a committee of nine ministers develop a paper on church organization and publish it in the *Review*.[46] That document appeared June 11. Among its recommendations was the formation of state or district conferences to regulate the work of the church in their respective territories.[47]

Reactions to the committee's recommendations were forceful in some sectors of the movement—especially in the East. Many of the eastern leaders apparently believed that White and those in the Midwest had apostatized from the truth in the area of organization.[48]

White, of course, took vigorous exception to the anti-organization faction. Reporting that "the brethren in Pennsylvania voted down organization, and the cause in Ohio has been dreadfully shaken," White summarized his feelings by writing that "*on our eastern tour thus far we seem to be wading through the influence of a stupid uncertainty upon the subject of organization.*" As a result, "instead of our being a unified people, growing stronger, we are in many places but little better than broken fragments, still scattering and growing weaker." "*How long shall we wait?*" he inquired of the *Review* readers.[49]

Ellen White was just as agitated on the topic of organization as her husband. She reported a vision on August 3, 1861, in which she was "shown that *some have feared that our churches would become Babylon if they should organize; but those in central New York have been perfect Babylon, confusion.* And now unless the churches are so organized that they can carry out and enforce order, they have nothing to hope for in the future; they must scatter into fragments."[50]

The time for action had arrived. Accordingly, a general meeting convened in Battle Creek from October 4 through 6, 1861, to form the first state conference. The October 1861 meeting is one of the pivotal events in Seventh-day Adventist history. The first item of business was "the proper manner of organizing churches." As a part of that item, James White recommended that the members of each congregation formally organize by signing a church covenant. "We, the undersigned," went his proposed covenant, "hereby associate ourselves together, as a church, taking the name, Seventh-day Adventists, covenanting to keep the commandments of God, and the faith of Jesus

Christ."[51]

The idea of signing a covenant stimulated a lengthy discussion. Moses Hull saw no problem in the idea since "we pledge ourselves only to do one thing, to keep the commandments of God and the faith of Jesus." "There can be," he added, "nothing more in Christianity.... No one can call this a creed or articles of faith."[52]

Loughborough then took the lead in discussing the dangers of a formal creed.

• "The first step of apostasy," he noted, "is to get up a creed, telling us what we shall believe.

• "The second is, to make that creed a test of fellowship.

• "The third is to try members by that creed.

• "The fourth to denounce as heretics those who do not believe that creed.

• "And, fifth, to commence persecution against such."[53]

James White also weighed into the discussion. "Making a creed," he declared, "is setting the stakes, and barring up the way to all future advancement." Those churches that had set up creeds "have marked out a course for the Almighty. They say virtually that the Lord must not do anything further than what has been marked out in the creed....The Bible is our creed. We reject everything in the form of a human creed. We take the Bible and the gifts of the Spirit; embracing the faith that thus the Lord will teach us from time to time. And in this we take a position against the formation of a creed. We are not taking one step, in what we are doing, toward becoming Babylon" [as oppression].[54]

The central item of business in the October 1861 meeting was the recommendation "to the churches in the State of Michigan to unite in one Conference, with the name of The Michigan Conference of Seventh-day Adventists." The delegates adopted the recommendation along with a simple structure consisting of a conference president, a conference clerk, and a conference committee of three.[55]

With the first state conference a reality, others quickly appeared in 1862: Southern Iowa (March 16), Northern Iowa (May 10), Vermont (June 15), Illinois (September 28), Wisconsin (September 28), Minnesota (October 4), and New York (October 25). But not all would follow Michigan's lead. An examination of the above list indicates that New England (with the exception of Vermont) was not represented. Some of the regions in that area would not form a local conference until 1870.

By 1862, however, the movement toward organization was rolling at full speed. That brings us to the third stage of the final drive.

While it is true that state conferences were in the process of being formed, the emerging denomination had no way to coordinate their work or the assignment of ministers to different fields. J. H. Waggoner raised that issue to consciousness in a forceful manner in June 1862. "I do not believe," he wrote, "that we shall ever fully realize the benefits of organization till this matter" of a general conference "is acted upon." He concluded his article by recommending that "every conference of Seventh-day Adventists send a delegate or delegates to the General Conference; and that a General Conference Committee be appointed, with whom the State conferences may correspond, and through whom they shall present their requests for laborers."[56]

Several readers of the *Review* responded to Waggoner's proposition with hearty affirmations in the summer of 1862. Without a general conference that shall represent the whole body of believers, J. N. Andrews argued, "we shall be thrown into confusion every time that concert of action is especially necessary. The work of organization, wherever it has been entered into in a proper manner, has borne good fruit; and hence I desire to see it completed in such a manner as shall secure its full benefit, not only to each church, but to the whole body of brethren and to the cause of truth."[57]

In October 1862 the Michigan Conference session not only set up operating procedures, but extended an invitation for "the several State Conferences to meet" with them "in general conference" at their 1863 annual meeting.[58] At James White's insistence the session was moved forward from October 1863 to May of that year. He believed it was imperative that the General Conference of Seventh-day Adventists form as soon as possible. Announcing the meeting in late April, White billed it as *"the most important meeting ever held by the Seventh-day Adventists."* As he saw it, *the proposed General Conference must be "the great regulator" of the state conferences if they were to secure "united, systematic action in the entire body" of believers.* The duty of the General Conference would be "to mark out the general course to be pursued by State Conferences." And if, White noted, "it be the pleasure of State Conferences to carry out the decisions of General Conference, unity thus far will be secured."[59]

The General Conference of Seventh-day Adventists organized at a meeting called for that purpose in Battle Creek from May 20 to May 23, 1863. The enabling action read: "For the purpose of securing unity and efficiency in labor, and promoting the general interests of the cause of present truth, and of perfecting the organization of the Seventh-day Adventists, we, the delegates from the several State Conferences, hereby proceed to organize a General Conference, and adopt the following constitution for the government thereof."[60]

The delegates unanimously elected James White president but he declined the invitation because some would interpret his forceful campaign for the establishment of a complete organization as a calculated grab for personal power. After some discussion, the session chose John Byington in White's place.[61]

Perspective

The battle for organization had been long and difficult, but by 1863 it was over. With a functional organization the denomination was ready to move forward. Looking back at the development of organization, three things stand out.

The first key element that allowed the anti-organizational people to organize was a transformation of their understanding of Babylon, which in the 1850s morphed from an idea associated with persecution to one highlighting confusion. James White repeatedly pointed out that without organization their confused state did not permit them to move forward. When others finally accepted the new connotation of Babylon, they were willing to organize, but only reluctantly. Their discussion of creedalism and its effects indicate their ongoing fear that Babylon as oppression could resurrect.

The second crucial understanding that allowed the Sabbatarians to organize was a transformed hermeneutic that had moved from one in which the only things permissible were those explicitly spelled out in the Bible to a hermeneutic that asserted that all things were lawful except those forbidden by the Bible, if they did not violate common sense. It is impossible to overestimate the impact of that transformation. Without it Adventism would have been a minor footnote to the history of New England and the American Midwest. But through it White provided the means by which he and his wife could guide the young movement into a mission to the entire world.

The third important understanding is that the move toward organization was fueled by a growing concept of mission. In fact, it was the pragmatic necessities of mission that undergirded every step in the organizational process and also the transformations of the budding movement's understanding of both Babylon and hermeneutics.

At bottom, mission to the world was the *only* reason for organization. And by the 1890s that mission had reached around the world. That very success would call for adjustments in 1901 so that the church could even be more effective in its worldwide outreach. And if the denomination is to remain effective in the 21st century, the logic of the 1860s and 1901 will have to continue to function in a rapidly growing, multiethnic church committed to the mission of taking the message of the three angels "to every nation, and kindred, and tongue, and people" (Revelation 14:6).

Notes

1. For more on the early development of Adventist organization, see Andrew G. Mustard, *James White and SDA Organization: Historical Development, 1844-1881* (Berrien Springs, MI: Andrews University Press, 1988); for a general overview of the development of Adventist organization, see George R. Knight, *Organizing for Mission and Growth: The Development of Adventist Church Structure* (Hagerstown, MD: Review and Herald Pub. Assn., 2006).

2. Joshua V. Himes, "Christian Connexion," in J. Newton Brown, ed., *Encyclopedia of Religious Knowledge* (Brattleboro, VT: Fessenden and Co., 1836), p. 362; italics supplied.

3. *Ibid.*, p. 363.

4. Charles Fitch, "'*Come Out of Her My People,*'" (Rochester, NY: E. Shepard's Press, 1843), pp. 9, 19, 24.

5. George Storrs, "Come Out of Her My People," *The Midnight Cry*, Feb. 15, 1844, pp. 237-238.

6. *Ibid.*, p. 238.

7. Ellen G. White, *Life Sketches of Ellen G. White* (Mountain View, CA: Pacific Press Pub. Assn., 1915), pp. 43-53.

8. James White to Bro. Bowles, Nov. 8, 1849; italics supplied.

9. Ellen G. White, *Spiritual Gifts* (Battle Creek, MI: James White, 1860), vol. 2, pp. 93, 97-99.

10. Ellen G. White, *Life Sketches of Ellen G. White*, p. 125.

11. James White to Bro. and Sis. Collins, Sept. 8, 1849; James White to My Dear Afflicted Brother, Mar. 18, 1850; Ellen G. White, "Vision at Paris Maine," MS 11, Dec. 25, 1850.

12. James White to Brethren in Christ, Nov. 11, 1851; [James White], "Our Tour East," *Review and Herald*, Nov. 25, 1851, p. 52. See also, Arthur L. White, *Ellen G. White: The Early Years, 1827-1862* (Washington, DC: Review and Herald Pub. Assn., 1985), pp. 216-226.

13. "F. M. Shimper to Bro. White," *Review and Herald*, Aug. 19, 1851, p. 15. See also, George R. Knight, "Early Seventh-day Adventists and Ordination, 1844-1863," in Nancy Vyhmeister, ed., *Women in Ministry: Biblical and Historical Perspectives* (Berrien Springs, MI: Andrews University Press, 1998), p. 106.

14. J. N. Loughborough, *The Church: Its Organization, Order and Discipline* ([Washington, DC]: Review and Herald, [1906]), p. 101.

15. [James White], "Gospel Order," *Review and Herald*, Dec. 6, 1853, p. 173; italics supplied.

16. Ellen G. White, *Early Writings* (Washington, DC: Review and Herald Pub. Assn., 1945), pp. 97, 99, 101; italics supplied.

17. [James White], "Gospel Order," *Review and Herald*, Mar. 28, 1854, p. 76.

18. Joseph Bates, "Church Order," *Review and Herald*, Aug. 29, 1854, pp. 22-23.

19. [James White], "Gospel Order," *Review and Herald*, Mar. 28, 1854, p. 76.

20. [James White], "Church Order," *Review and Herald*, Jan. 23, 1855, p. 164.

21. J. B. Frisbie, "Church Order," *Review and Herald*, Dec. 26, 1854, p. 147.

22. J. B. Frisbie, "Church Order," *Review and Herald*, Jan. 9, 1855, p. 155.

23. Joseph Bates, "Church Order," *Review and Herald*, Aug. 29, 1854, p. 22; italics supplied.

24. Uriah Smith, "To the Friends of the Review," *Review and Herald*, Dec. 4, 1855, p. 76; James White to Brother Dodge, Aug. 20, 1855.

25. J. N. Loughborough, *Rise and Progress of the Seventh-day Adventists* (Battle Creek, MI: General Conf. Association of the Seventh-day Adventists, 1892), p. 208.

26. For an overview of the Systematic Benevolence plan see Brian Strayer, "'Sister Betsy' and Systematic Giving among Adventists," *Adventist Review*, Dec. 6, 1984, pp. 8-10.

27. Ellen G. White, *Testimonies for the Church* (Mountain View, CA: Pacific Press Pub. Assn., 1948), vol. 1, p. 191.

28. James White, "A Complaint," *Review and Herald*, June 16, 1859, p. 28.

29. A. S. Hutchins, "Church Order," *Review and Herald*, Sept. 18, 1856, p. 158; J. B. Frisbie, "Church Order," *Review and Herald*, Oct. 23, 1856, p. 198.

30. James White, "Conference Address," *Review and Herald*, June 9, 1859, pp. 21-23; Joseph Bates and Uriah Smith, "Business Proceedings," *ibid.*, pp. 20-21.

31. James White, "Yearly Meetings," *Review and Herald*, July 21, 1859, p. 68;

italics supplied.

32. *Ibid.*

33. *Ibid.*; italics supplied.

34. *Ibid.*

35. *Ibid.*

36. *Ibid.*

37. James White, "Borrowed Money," *Review and Herald*, Feb. 23, 1860, p. 108.

38. R. F. Cottrell, "Making Us a Name," *Review and Herald*, Mar. 22, 1860, pp. 140-141.

39. James White, "'Making Us a Name,'" *Review and Herald*, Mar. 29, 1860, p. 152.

40. James White, "'Making Us a Name,'" *Review and Herald*, Apr. 26, 1860, pp. 180-182.

41. Ellen G. White, *Testimonies*, vol. 1, p. 211.

42. Godfrey T. Anderson, "Make Us a Name," *Adventist Heritage*, July 1974, p. 30.

43. James White, in "Business Proceedings of B. C. Conference," *Review and Herald*, Oct. 16, 1860, p. 169.

44. *Ibid.*, pp. 170-171.

45. Joseph Bates and Uriah Smith, "Business Proceedings of B. C. Conference," *Review and Herald*, Oct. 23, 1860, p. 179.

46. Joseph Bates and Uriah Smith, "Business Proceedings of B. C. Conference," *Review and Herald*, Apr. 30, 1861, p. 189.

47. J. H. Waggoner et al., "Conference Address," *Review and Herald*, June 11, 1861, p. 21.

48. [James White], "Eastern Tour," *Review and Herald*, Sept. 3, 1861, p. 108.

49. [James White], "Organization," *Review and Herald*, Aug. 27, 1861, p. 100; italics supplied.

50. Ellen G. White, *Testimonies*, vol. 1, p. 270; italics supplied.

51. Joseph Bates and Uriah Smith, "Doings of the Battle Creek Conference, Oct. 5 & 6, 1861," *Review and Herald*, Oct. 8, 1861, p. 148.

52. *Ibid.*

53. *Ibid.*

54. *Ibid.*

55. *Ibid.*

56. J. H. Waggoner, "General Conferences," *Review and Herald*, June 24, 1862, p. 29.

57. J. N. Andrews, "General Conferences," *Review and Herald*, July 15, 1862, p. 52.

58. Joseph Bates and Uriah Smith, "Business Proceedings of the Michigan State Conference," *Review and Herald*, Oct. 14, 1862, p. 157.

59. [James White], "General Conference," *Review and Herald*, Apr. 28, 1863, p. 172; italics supplied.

60. John Byington and Uriah Smith, "Report of General Conference of Seventh-day Adventists," *Review and Herald*, May 26, 1863, pp. 204-206.

61. *Ibid.*

CHAPTER TWO

The Role of Union Conferences in Relation to Higher Authorities[1*]

There are only two truly Catholic churches in the world today: the Roman Catholic and the Adventist catholic.

Now that I have your attention, I trust that you realize that the primary meaning of the word "catholic" is "universal."

Adventism is catholic in the sense that it has a worldwide commission to fulfill—the mission of the three angels of Revelation 14 to take the end-time message to every nation, tongue, and people.

Perhaps the major difference between the Roman brand of Catholicism and the Adventist variety is the issue of authority. For Rome it is a top-down proposition. For Adventism it has traditionally been from the bottom up. I say traditionally because some Adven-

---

* The present chapter was developed as a presentation for the "Leadership Summit on Mission and Governance" sponsored by the Columbia Union Conference in March 2016. The stimulus for the meetings was the fact that the Columbia Union Conference had been ordaining women to ministry and was therefore out of harmony with the General Conference as expressed in the 2015 session vote.

tists seem to be in the valley of decision on this most important of all ecclesiastical issues. The real question facing the denomination is How catholic do we really want to be?

Expanded Mission Demands a Reorganization

In my first chapter, I highlighted how the anti-organizational people finally managed to organize in the face of the needs of mission. However, in order to do that they had to see that Babylon not only meant oppression but also confusion. And, more importantly, they had to move from a literalistic hermeneutic that held that the only things permissible were those specifically spelled out in Scripture to one in which everything was permissible that did not contradict the Bible and was in harmony with common sense. In the end they organized churches, local conferences, and a general conference in 1861/1863 for the purpose of mission, but with a cautious eye on higher ecclesiastical authorities removing their freedom in Christ. That potential problem would be highlighted in 1888 when a powerful General Conference president sought to block the preaching of righteousness by faith by Jones and Waggoner.

The 1860 organization worked well, and Adventism and its institutions by the end of the 1890s had spread around the world. In fact, the church of 1863 with its 3,500 members (all in North America), one institution, eight conferences, and about 30 ministers could hardly be compared to the denomination of 1900, which was not only worldwide but had dozens of healthcare facilities, more than 200 schools, and other institutions.

But growth had brought its own pains and problems to the ever-expanding movement. By the 1890s two major problems in the 1860s organization had surfaced: (1) too much control by the General

Conference over the local conferences and (2) too little control over the auxiliary organizations, such as those that supervised the medical and educational work of the denomination.

The first of those issues related most clearly to the geographical spread of the denomination. That problem was aggravated by the stand taken by the General Conference presidents. G. I. Butler, for example, in the late 1880s noted in connection with the formation of the General Conference Association that General Conference "supervision embraces all its interests in every part of the world. There is not an institution among us, not a periodical issued, not a Conference or society, not a mission field connected with our work, that it has not a right to advise and counsel and investigate. *It is the highest authority of an earthly character among Seventh-day Adventists.*"[2] O. A. Olsen took the same position in 1894 when he wrote that "it is the province of the General Conference carefully to watch over, and have a care for, the work in every part of the field. The General Conference, therefore, is not only acquainted with the needs and conditions of every Conference, but it understands these needs and conditions as they stand related to every other Conference and mission field.... It may also be thought that those in charge of local interests have a deeper interest in, and carry a greater responsibility for, the local work, than the General Conference can possibly do. Such can hardly be the case, if the General Conference does its duty. The General Conference stands as it were in the place of the parent to the local conference."[3]

That mentality in essence held that the General Conference needed to be consulted on all issues of importance. It may have sounded like a nice idea, but in practice it didn't work. That problem is nicely illustrated by A. G. Daniells speaking to the issue from the perspective of 1913. Before the adoption of the union conferences, he noted, every decision that transcended the decision-making responsibility of a local conference had to be referred to headquarters in Battle Creek. The problem was that at its best the mail took four weeks each direction from Australia and often arrived to find the members of the General Conference Executive Committee away from their offices. "I remember," Daniels noted, "that we have waited three or four months before we could get any reply to our questions." And even then it might be a five- or six-line inquiry saying that the General Conference officers really didn't understand the issue and needed further information. And so it went until "after six or nine months, perhaps, we would get the matter settled."[4]

Ellen White took the lead in combating the centralization of authority in the General Conference. In 1883, for example, she wrote that the leading administrators had made a mistake in "each one" thinking "that he was the very one who must bear all the responsibilities" and give others "no chance" to develop their God-given skills.[5] During the 1880s and 1890s she repeatedly advocated localized decision making on the grounds that the leaders in Battle Creek could not possibly understand the situation as well as people on site. As she put it in 1896, "the men at Battle Creek are no more inspired to give unerring advice than are the men in other places, to whom the Lord has entrusted the work in their locality."[6] A year earlier she had written that the *"work of God" had been "retarded by criminal unbelief in [God's] power to use the common people to carry forward His work successfully."*[7]

By the end of the 1890s Ellen White would be thundering against the "kingly power" that the leaders in Battle Creek had taken to themselves. In one fascinating testimony in 1895 she wrote that "the high-handed power that has been developed, as though position has made men gods, makes me afraid, and ought to cause fear. It is a curse wherever and by whomsoever it is exercised. This lording it over God's heritage will create such a disgust of man's jurisdiction that a state of insubordination will result." She went on to state that the "only safe course is to remove" such leaders since "all ye are brethren," lest "great harm be done."[8]

Erich Baumgartner, in his study of the issues surrounding reorganization, summed up the problem by noting that "the most urgent of the many problems were connected to an ever widening discrepancy between world wide church growth during the 1880's and 1890's and the narrow, inflexible, central organizational base of the SDA church located in Battle Creek."[9] That inflexible centralized authority prevented adaptation to local needs. As Ellen White put it, "the place, the circumstances, the interest, the moral sentiment of the people, will have to decide in many cases the course of action to be pursued" and that "those who are right on the ground are to decide what shall be done."[10]

The denomination struggled throughout the 1890s to find a solution to the problem. The first attempt began in November 1888 with the creation of four districts in North America. By 1893 there would be six in North America and one each in Australasia and Europe. But the district system essentially operated as divisions of the General Conference, with each district leader being a member of the General Conference Committee. Beyond that, the districts had no constituency or legislative authority.[11] In short, they were not effective.

A more helpful solution was the development of a union conference by W. C. White in Australia in 1894. That act was resisted by O. A. Olsen, the General Conference president, who told the General

Conference Executive Committee that "he thought nothing should be planned so as to interfere with the general supervision and work legitimately belonging to the General Conference, as that is the highest organized authority under God on the earth."[12]

But White, the leader for the Australasian district, and his colleague Arthur G. Daniells were in a tight spot and needed to do something. That led to the appointment of a committee that developed the first union conference constitution, which was approved on January 19, 1894, appointing White and Daniells president and secretary, respectively.

That move was not accomplished with the help of the General Conference but in spite of its counsel. Years later Daniells reported that not everyone was happy with the union conference idea. *"Some of our brethren thought then that the work was going to be wrecked,* that we were going to tear the organization all to pieces, and get up secession out there in the South Sea islands." But in actuality, he observed, the result was quite the opposite. The new organizational approach greatly facilitated the mission of the church in the South Pacific, while the new Australasian Union Conference remained a loyal and integral part of the General Conference system.[13]

That move was revolutionary. Barry Oliver in his massive study of the 1901/1903 reorganization, notes that "the Australasian experiment represented the first time that a level of organization other than a local conference or the General Conference had a constituency— that is, it had executive powers which were granted by the levels of organization 'below' it, and not by the General Conference."[14]

The second issue troubling the church during the 1890s was the legally independent auxiliary organizations that had developed in Battle Creek, including the Publishing Association, the General Tract and Missionary Society, the Educational Society, the General Sabbath School Association, the Health and Temperance Association, the General Conference Association, the Religious Liberty Association, and the Foreign Mission Board. Legally each was independent, and there was no effective way to coordinate their work.

That was bad enough, but A. T. Robinson, president of the newly formed South African Conference, discovered in 1892 that he did not even have enough personnel to staff all of the organizations. Out of necessity, Robinson decided that he would not create independent organizations but would develop departments under the leadership of the conference. Both Olsen and W. C. White felt concern over the suggestion, Olsen fearing that the plan contained "elements of danger in too much centralization." The General Conference leadership eventually told Robinson not to develop departments. But it was too late. Because of the large amount of time it took to communicate, Robinson had already instituted the program and found that it worked.[15]

In 1898 Robinson moved to Australia where he became president of the Victoria Conference. There he presented the idea to Daniells and W. C. White, who rejected it. But Robinson's local conference leaders had already accepted the idea on principle and voted it into being. Before the turn of the century both Daniells and White had adopted the departmental concept and helped it find a place throughout the various conferences in the Australasia Union.[16]

With that move the stage had been set for the reorganization of the denomination at the 1901 General Conference session. *Let it be remembered that both of the major innovations were developed in response to regional mission needs and both were developed in opposition to General Conference pronouncements and procedures.* But they worked. The major lesson is that without the freedom to experiment

Adventism would not have its present system of organization.

The Reorganization of 1901

The tone for the 1901 General Conference session was set for it on April 1, the day before the conference officially began. On that date Daniells chaired a meeting of denominational leaders in the Battle Creek College library. The major presenter was Ellen White, who in no uncertain terms called for "new blood" and an "entire new organization" that broadened the governing base of the denomination. Opposing the centralization of power in a few individuals, she left no doubt that "kingly, ruling power" and "any administrator who had a 'little throne' would have to go." She called for a "renovation without any delay. To have this Conference pass on and close up as the Conferences have done, with the same manipulating, with the very same tone and the same order—God forbid! God forbid, brethren."[17]

She repeated the same sentiments on the first day of the session, noting that "God has not put any kingly power in our ranks to control this or that branch of the work. *The work has been greatly restricted by the efforts to control it in every line....* If the work had not been so restricted by an impediment here, and an impediment there, and on the other side an impediment, it would have gone forward in its majesty."[18]

The key word in seeking to understand the 1901 session is "decentralization." Some of the most important changes at the conference were the authorization to create union conferences and union missions in all parts of the world, the discontinuation of the auxiliary organizations as independent associations and their integration into the conference administrative structure, and the transfer of ownership and management of institutions that had been under General Conference jurisdiction to the respective unions and their local conferences.

The unions, Daniells noted, were created with "large committees, and full authority and power to deal with all matters within their boundaries."[19] And Ellen White pointed out that *"it has been a necessity to organize union conferences, that the General Conference shall not exercise dictation over all the separate conferences."*[20]

On the basis of those and other statements, the late Gerry Chudleigh has argued that the unions "were created to act as *firewalls* between the GC and the conferences, making 'dictation' impossible." He buttressed his firewall image with two major points. First, "each union had its own constitution and bylaws and was to be governed by its own constituency." And, second, "the officers of each union were to be elected by their own union constituency, and, therefore, could not be controlled, replaced or disciplined by the GC."[21]

"To put as bluntly as possible," Chudleigh wrote, "after 1901, the General Conference could vote whatever it wanted unions and conferences to do, or not do, but the unions and conferences were autonomous and could do what they believed would best advance the work of God in their fields. The GC executive committee, or the General Conference in business session, could vote to fire a union president or conference president, or vote to merge a union or conference with another one, but their vote would change nothing: the union or conference would still exist and the member delegates could elect whomever they wanted as president."[22] A case in point in contemporary Adventism is the Southeastern California Conference, which has an ordained female president, in spite of the wishes of the General Conference. Some in the General Conference, in the words of Ellen White, have tried to "dictate" that she be removed. But there is nothing that they have been able to do about the situation. The firewall is in place.

Ellen White was thrilled with the results of the 1901 session with its creation of union conferences. To her unions were "in the order of God." Near the close of the 1901 session she noted that "I was never more astonished in my life than at the turn things have taken in this meeting. This is not our work. God has brought it about."[23] And some months later she wrote that "during the General Conference the Lord wrought mightily for His people. Every time I think of that meeting, a sweet solemnity comes over me, and sends a glow of gratitude to my soul. We have seen the stately stepping of the Lord our Redeemer."[24]

She was especially gratified that freedom of action had been opened up and that the General Conference would not be in a position to "exercise dictation over all the separate conferences." Along that line, she noted near the close of the 1901 session that "I earnestly hope that those laboring in the fields to which you are going will not think that you and they can not labor together, unless your minds run in the same channels as theirs, unless you view things exactly as they view them."[25] Early on Daniells held the same position. While he saw *the General Conference as fostering the work in all parts of the world, "it cannot be the brains, and conscience, and mouthpiece for our brethren in these different countries."*[26]

Looking back from the perspective of 1903, in his opening address to the session Daniells was gratified that major decision-making authority had been distributed to those "who are on the ground" and understood the needs of the various fields. "Many can testify that the blessing of God has attended the efforts that have been made to distribute responsibilities, and thus transfer the care, perplexity, and management that once centered in Battle Creek to all parts of the world, where they belong."[27]

At the close of the 1901 session all looked good. Autonomous unions had transferred authority from the General Conference to local leaders and the creation of departments had transferred authority over the auxillary organizations to church leaders at all levels. It appeared that the denomination had captured the elusive goal of unity in diversity so that it might most effectively minister to the needs of varying cultures around the world.

The 1903 General Conference and the
Threat to Unity in Diversity

By early 1903 Ellen White's euphoria at the close of the 1901 session had disappeared. In January she wrote that "the result of the last General Conference has been the greatest, the most terrible sorrow of my life. No change was made. *The spirit that should have been brought into the whole work as the result of that meeting was not brought in.*" Many "carried into their work the wrong principles that had been prevailing in the work at Battle Creek."[28]

When she said that "no change was made" she was speaking on the spiritual rather than the organizational level. The major problem was that the old denominational demon of "kingly power" had reasserted its ugly head.

At this point we need to go back and take a closer look at the denomination's auxiliary organizations. In the monopolistic spirit of the times each was seeking to control all the institutions around the world from the institutions in Battle Creek. Thus the Review and Herald was seeking to control all other publishing houses, W. W. Prescott was not only head of the Adventist Educational Association but also president of three colleges simultaneously, and John Harvey Kellogg was seeking worldwide control through the Medical Missionary and Benevolent Association and the massive Battle Creek Sanitarium. As a result, "kingly power" was not merely a problem of the General Conference president but also of the leaders of the various independent organizations.

The reorganization in 1901 had largely taken care of the problem through its development of the departmental system and its transfer of the ownership of institutional properties to the various levels of the church. But there was one glaring exception to that success: Namely, Kellogg and his medical empire, which had more employees than all other sectors of the church combined and had been granted roughly one fourth of the positions on the General Conference Executive Committee in 1901. It didn't take long for the assertive Kellogg to run into a struggle with the equally adamant Daniells, the new president of the General Conference. The struggle itself was nothing new. The doctor had always jealously guarded his sector of the Adventist pie. He had no use for any church leaders who attempted to block the development of his program. As early as 1895 we find him referring to conference presidents as "little popes." But by 1903, as C. H. Parsons put it, Kellogg filled "the position of pope completely" in the medical program.[29]

That was bad enough. But, unfortunately, Daniells in his drive to bring Kellogg and his associates into line had by 1903 resurrected tendencies to "kingly power" in the presidential office. That development was natural enough. After all, power generally has to be met by power. But Ellen White was distraught at the development. On April 3 in the testimony in which she noted that unions had been organized so that the General Conference could not "exercise dictation over all the separate conferences" she again raised

the topic of "kingly authority" and noted that "the General Conference has fallen into strange ways, and we have reason to marvel that
judgment has not fallen" on it.[30]

Nine days later she wrote to Daniells himself, telling him that he
needed to "be careful how we press our opinions upon those whom
God has instructed.... Brother Daniells, God would not have you suppose that you can exercise a kingly power over your brethren."[31] That
was not the last rebuke she would send him. The years to come would
see similar counsel to him and others in leadership.[32]

*One of the casualties of the struggle between Kellogg and Daniells
in 1902 and 1903 was the careful balance of unity in diversity that had
been achieved in 1901.* Ellen White back in 1894 had set forth "unity
in diversity" as "God's plan," with unity being achieved by each aspect
of the work being connected to Christ the vine.[33] In 1901 and early
1902 Daniells had championed that ideal, noting in 1902 to the European Union Conference that just "because a thing is done in a certain
way in one place is not reason why it should be done in the same way
in another place, or even in the same place at the same time."[34]

But that ideal began to give way by late 1902 as the Kellogg forces
sought to unseat Daniells and replace him with A. T. Jones, who was
by that time in the doctor's camp.[35] In that struggle the Kellogg/Jones
forces were pushing for diversity. That dynamic impelled Daniells to
emphasize unity as he moved toward a more authoritative stance.
Thus the delicate balance related to unity in diversity lost out soon
after the 1901 session. And, as Oliver points out, *unity at the expense
of diversity has been the focus of the General Conference ever since the
1902 crisis.*[36]

Yet, Oliver notes in his very sophisticated discussion of the topic, *in the long run "unity is dependent on the recognition of diversity,"*

and that *we should see the denomination's diversity as a tool to help the church reach an extremely diverse world.* From Oliver's perspective, Adventism in the 21st century is one of the most ethnically and culturally diverse groups in the world. Diversity is a fact that cannot be suppressed. "If diversity is neglected, the church will be unable to perform its task.... The church which subordinates the need to recognize diversity to a demand for unity is denying the very means by which it is best equipped to accomplish the task.... The issue for the Seventh-day Adventist Church is whether or not unity is to be regarded as that organizing principle whose importance eclipses that of all other principles." "A commitment to a doctrine of unity which imposes alien forms on any group, when adequate Christian forms could be derived from within the culture of the group itself, does not enhance unity." Oliver prods us a bit when he suggests that what Adventists need to ask themselves is whether their goal is unity or mission.[37]

Before moving away from the topic of unity in diversity it should be noted that unity and uniformity are not the same thing. Some have argued that Adventism must be united in mission, its core message, and in servanthood, but not in everything. In fact, these persons suggest that many issues need to be decided by locality and even by individuals. A movement can be united without being uniform. Unfortunately, in the drive for unity the General Conference has too often failed to note that distinction. One size fits all is too often the goal. In the process it has spawned disunity among various cultural groups.

One of the purposes of the 1901 reorganization was to foster localized decision making that could contribute to the ideal of unity in diversity through what Chudleigh called the union conference "firewall." Chudleigh in his thought-provoking *Who Runs the Church?* illustrates how the General Conference has progressively sought to weaken the firewall of autonomous unions through official actions that have sought to make unions obligated to follow all policies and programs and initiatives "adopted and approved by the General Conference of Seventh-day Adventists in its quinquennial sessions" and by taking initiatives and making pronouncements in areas that church members and even leaders have come to believe are within its rightful jurisdiction even if they are not. Since such actions are largely accepted without question, Chudleigh concludes that "the more well-accepted a GC initiative is, the more it contributes to members believing the Seventh-day Adventist Church is hierarchical."[38]

The General Conference as the Highest Authority on Earth

Tensions between the authority of the General Conference and that of the local conferences have existed from early in the history of organized Adventism. In August 1873, in the context of a lack of respect for General Conference officers, James White noted that "our General Conference is the highest earthly authority with our people, and is designed to take charge of the entire work in this and all other countries."[39] Then in 1877 the General Conference in session voted that "the highest authority under God among Seventh-day Adventists is found in the will of the body of that people, as expressed in the decisions of the General Conference *when acting within its proper jurisdiction*; and that such decisions should be submitted to by all without exception, *unless they can be shown to conflict with the word of God and the rights of individual conscience.*"[40]

That vote seems clear enough and both of the Whites accepted it. Please note, however, that it did highlight limitations related to the "proper jurisdiction" of the General Conference and "the rights of individual conscience." We will return to both of those items below.

So the matter of the authority of the General Conference was settled. Or was it? Ellen White would make some interesting statements on the topic in the 1890s. In 1891, for example, she wrote that "I was obliged to take the position that there was not the voice of God in the General Conference management and decisions.... Many of the positions taken, going forth as the voice of the General Conference, have been the voice of one, two, or three men who were misleading the Conference."[41] Again in 1896 she noted that the General Conference "is no longer the voice of God."[42] And in 1901 she wrote that "the people have lost confidence in those who have management of the work. Yet we hear that the voice of the [General] Conference is the voice of God. Every time I have heard this, I have thought it was almost blasphemy. The voice of the conference ought to be the voice of God, but it is not."[43]

An analysis of those negative statements indicates that they refer to occasions when the General Conference did not act as a representative body, when its decision-making authority was centralized in a person or a few people, or when the General Conference had not been following sound principles.[44] That conclusion lines up with Ellen White's statements across time. In fact, she specifically spoke to the point in a manuscript read before the delegates of the 1909 General Conference session in which she responded to the schismatic activities of A. T. Jones and others. "At times," she told the delegates, "when a small group of men entrusted with the general management of the work have, in the name of the General Conference, sought to carry out unwise plans and to restrict God's work, I have said that I could no longer regard the voice of the General Conference, represented by these few men, as the voice of God. But this is not saying that the decisions of a General Conference composed of an assembly of duly appointed, representative men from all parts of the field should not be respected. God has ordained that the representatives of His church from all parts of the earth, when assembled in a General Conference, shall have authority."[45]

So the matter is settled. Or is it? Has the General Conference in session evolved beyond the stage of fallibility as God's voice? Does an official vote of a worldwide conclave have something akin to papal infallibility? Some wonder.

Chief among the wonderers in 2017 are the church's young adults in the developed nations, many of them well-educated professionals. In all honesty and sincerity they are not only asking questions, but many are deeply disturbed.

How, some of them want to know, does the voice of God operate when it is widely reported that delegates in some unions in at least two divisions on two continents were told in no uncertain terms how to vote on such issues as women's ordination, knowing that they could face a grilling if the secret vote went wrong? They wonder how Ellen White would see such maneuvering in relation to the voice of God.

And these young adults wonder about the booing and heckling of Jan Paulsen when he raised issues related to ordination with no immediate, significant public rebuke by the denomination's highest authorities. One can only wonder how Ellen White would factor the voice of God into such dynamics, or whether she would have seen shades of Minneapolis.

Thoughtful young adults also wonder how serious the General

Conference president himself is in interpreting *all* of the voted-in-session actions as being the voice of God. A widely publicized case in point took place on Sabbath, November 11, 2011, in Melbourne, Australia. The Victoria Conference had planned a city-wide regional meeting, which would feature the General Conference president. Part of the day's activities included the ordination of two men and the commissioning of one woman in a united service. Both the ordaining and the commissioning were in line with General Conference policy, but the General Conference president insisted at the last minute that the integrated service be divided into two separate services: one for ordination and the other for commissioning, so that he could participate only in the service for the two males without having to be associated with the commissioning.

Now young adult thinking at its best would have to grant the president the right of conscience to not participate in the commissioning of a female if he did not believe in it. In fact, that appears to be in line with the ruling of the 1877 General Conference session that respected "the rights of individual conscience" even in the face of a "highest authority under God" vote by the General Conference in session.[46] That is clear enough. But to thinking people it has raised related questions. For example, if the General Conference president can choose not to line up with a session-voted policy, might they do the same thing on the basis of conscience? More seriously, why couldn't an entire union constituency act on the same conscience-based rationale? Many have viewed the actions of the denomination's president as having set a precedent in taking a step that put him out of harmony with the policy of the world church.

Other questions have surfaced in the minds of the denomination's young adults. One has to do with the "rumor" that some of the top denominational leadership would like to reverse the General Conference actions that have allowed for the ordination of local female elders and the commissioning of female pastors. What does that tell us about the "voice of God" votes? That some are wrong? And if some are mistakes, how do we know which ones?

And, finally, some have wondered if Adventism might have a problem in that it has developed a polity for the world church based on democratic procedures in a population in which most of the voters come from countries that lack a truly functional democratic heritage and where top down commands even affect secret voting. And, given the small proportion of votes in North America, Europe, and Australia, they wonder if the special needs of those fields ever will be able to be met unless they are voted on by the majority of the church, which may not understand the situations or even care about them.

It appears that in 2017 the dynamics of 1901 have been turned on their head. Then the problem was North America not being sensitive to the needs of the mission fields. Now it is the former mission fields not being sensitive to the needs of North America. And with that issue we have returned to the role of unions and why they were created in the first place: because people on location understand their needs better than people at a distance.

A Contemporary Illustration of the Tension Between Unions and Higher Authorities

It should not come as a surprise to anyone reading this that the most serious issue related to the tension between union conferences and the General Conference in 2017 is the question of the ordination of women to the gospel ministry. I do not want to spend much time on this issue, but it would not be totally responsible for me to neglect the topic.

Before moving into the issue itself, it should be noted that the recently voted Adventist position on ordination is a problem for many evangelicals and others. For example, one Wheaton College biblical scholar recently told one of my friends that he could not understand how a denomination that had a female prophet as its most influential clergy person could take such a stand. The vote in such people's minds is either a sign of hypocrisy or a breakdown of logic or both.

Here we need to look at some basic facts. After all, female ordination

- is not a biblical issue (years of study on the topic have not created consensus and neither will repeated votes),
- is not a Spirit of Prophecy issue, and
- is not a General Conference policy issue.

That last point has been widely misunderstood. At no time has the Seventh-day Adventist Church specified a gender qualification for ordination.[47] The General Conference Secretariat has recently argued otherwise on the basis of male gender language used in the *Working Policy's* discussion of qualifications for ordination.[48] But, as Gary Patterson has pointed out, "the working policy was filled with male gender language until the 1980s when it was decided to change its wording to gender neutral. An editorial group was assigned the task, and made the changes. The fact that they changed all the rest of the document, but not the wording in the ordination section does not constitute a policy, unless it is listed in the criteria for ordination, which it notably is not." The editorial decision, Patterson points out, was based on precedent or tradition since all ordained ministers up to that time had been male.[49] And while tradition in itself may be good enough for the Roman branch of catholicism, it has never held authoritative weight in Adventism. If the Secretariat's argument is viewed as conclusive, then we have editors developing binding policy for the world church rather than a vote at a General Conference session. That, needless to say, has serious implications.

At this point we need to return to the General Conference action of 1877 that stipulated that a vote of a General Conference session is the highest authority on earth "when acting within its proper jurisdiction."[50] Since the selection of who to ordain was in the 1860s made a prerogative of the conferences and in the early 1900s was transferred to the unions, it does not fall into the jurisdiction of the General Conference. Thus rulings by the General Conference on the gender issue are outside its jurisdiction until an action is taken to make gender a requirement for ordination. From that perspective, the unions in the North American Division made a major mistake when they asked the General Conference for permission to ordain women. Rather, the unions should have followed the logic of James White, who repeatedly noted that all things are lawful that do not contradict Scripture and are in harmony with common sense.[51]

Before moving away from the topic of policy, we need to listen to another point made by Gary Patterson. "There is," he wrote, "a perception existing that the General Conference cannot violate policy, that whatever it does constitutes policy, but this is not so. The General Conference can violate policy just as well as any other level of the church, if and when it acts contrary to the provisions of policy. Unless and until the General Conference changes its policy by vote, any action contrary to that policy is a violation. Thus, the unions are not out of policy on this matter of gender inclusiveness in the ordination of ministers. The General Conference itself is out of policy by intruding where it does not have authority."[52]

At the 1990 General Conference session the denomination officially voted not to ordain women to the gospel ministry because of "the possible risk of disunity, dissension, and diversion from the mission of the church."[53] That was 27 years ago and *the passage of time has demonstrated that unity can be fractured from more than one direction.* It is no longer a question of dividing the church and hindering mission. THE CHURCH IS ALREADY DIVIDED. And whether those inside of the moat recognize it or not, significant numbers of young adults are leaving the church over the issue even as many more, while still attending, have tuned out the authority of the church.

The denomination needs to see that this problem will not simply disappear. Somewhat like the issue of slavery in the United States from the 1820s to the 1860s, the ordination of women will stay on the agenda no matter how much money is spent in studying the topic and no matter how many votes are taken. Without adequate scriptural grounding, legislation at the worldwide level of the General Conference will not and cannot bring resolution.

And once again we are back to the reason that unions were created in 1901. Namely, that the people on the ground are best able to decide how to facilitate mission in their areas. And *here I might suggest that the real issue in 2017 is not the ordination of women but the role of union conferences.* The ordination problem is only a surface issue. But it is one that cannot be avoided. And here I need to backtrack from a position I suggested to the annual leadership seminar of the North American Division in December 2012. At that time I noted that the problem could be solved by just doing away with the word "ordination" (which in the sense we use it is not biblical) and just commission all pastors regardless of gender. But I have come to see that as a copout and an avoidance of the real issue of the relation between unions and the General Conference.

That thought brings me to my final point.

There Is an Authority Higher Than That of the General Conference

Here we need to remember the title of this chapter: "The Role of Union Conferences in Relation to Higher Authorities"—plural. While the General Conference in session may be the highest authority *on earth*, there is yet a higher authority *in heaven*. Ellen White made that point when she wrote in 1901 that "men are not capable of ruling the church. God is our Ruler."[54]

With that in mind, we need to briefly mention several points:

1. It is God through the Holy Spirit who calls pastors and equips them with spiritual gifts (Ephesians 4:11). The church does not call a pastor.

2. Ordination as we know it is not a biblical concept, but one developed in the history of the early church and, notes Ellen White, was eventually "greatly abused" and "unwarrantable importance was attached to the act."[55]

3. The laying on of hands, however, is a biblical concept and served in the Bible, according to *The Acts of the Apostles,* as a "public recognition" that God had already called the recipients. By that ceremony no power or qualification was added to the ordinands.[56] Over time, the early church began to call the ceremony of laying on of hands an ordination service. But "the English word 'ordination,' to which we have become accustomed, derives not from any Greek word used in the New Testament, but from the Latin *ordinare.*"[57]

4. The Seventh-day Adventist Church recognizes God's call of

both males and females to the pastoral ministry by the laying on of hands. That is biblical. BUT it calls the dedication of males "ordination" and that for females "commissioning." That is not biblical. Rather, it is merely a word game that apparently has medieval concepts of ordination at its root since there is certainly no grounding for it in either the Bible or Ellen White's writings.

And here we are back to the question I raised at the beginning of this chapter. Are we happy being catholic in the traditional Adventist sense or do we prefer the Roman type? When any organization, including Adventism, begins to impose nonbiblical ideas contrary to such biblical ones as pastoral calling and the laying on of hands in recognition of God's call, it may be coming perilously close to replicating some of the most serious mistakes of Roman Catholicism.

Here Matthew 18:18 is informative. From the perspective of Rome the idea is that whatever the church votes on earth is ratified in heaven. But the Greek in the verse actually says that "whatever you bind on the earth will have been bound in heaven" (cf. NASB). *The Seventh-day Adventist Bible Commentary* has it correct when it notes that "even here Heaven's ratification of the decision on earth will take place only if the decision is made in harmony with the principles of heaven."[58] It is God who calls. All the church can do is recognize that call through the biblical act of laying on of hands.

After 115 years Adventism is still faced with the twin Romish temptations of kingly power and top-down authority. But unlike the church before the 1901 reorganization, the denomination now has the machinery in place to effectively reject the challenge. Yet it remains for some future historian to report on whether 21st-century Adventism decided to use or neglect that machinery.

Notes

1. For more on the development of union conferences, see Barry David Oliver, *SDA Organizational Structure: Past, Present and Future* (Berrien Springs, MI: Andrews University Press, 1989); for an overview of the development of Adventist organization, see George R. Knight, *Organizing for Mission and Growth: The Development of Adventist Church Structure* (Hagerstown, MD: Review and Herald Pub. Assn., 2006).

2. [George I. Butler], *Seventh-day Adventist Year Book: 1888* (Battle Creek, MI: Review and Herald Publishing House, 1889), p. 50, cited in Oliver, p. 58; italics supplied.

3. O. A. Olsen, "The Movements of Laborers," *Review and Herald*, June 12, 1894, p. 379.

4. *General Conference Bulletin*, May 23, 1913, p. 108.

5. Ellen G. White to W. C. and Mary White, Aug. 23, 1883.

6. Ellen G. White to W. W. Prescott and Wife, Sept. 1, 1896.

7. Ellen G. White, "The Great Need of the Holy Spirit," *Review and Herald*, July 16, 1895, p. 450; italics supplied.

8. Ellen G. White, *Special Testimonies: Series A* (Payson, AZ: Leaves-of-Autumn, n.d.) pp. 299-300.

9. Erich Baumgartner, "Church Growth and Church Structure: 1901 Reorganization in the Light of the Expanding Missionary Enterprise of the SDA Church," Seminar Paper, Andrews University, 1987, p. 66.

10. Ellen G. White to Ministers of the Australian Conference, Nov. 11, 1894; E. G. White, *General Conference Bulletin*, 1901, p. 70.

11. See Knight, *Organizing*, pp. 81-83.

12. General Conference Committee Minutes, Jan. 25, 1893.

13. *General Conference Bulletin*, May 23, 1913, p. 108; italics supplied.

14. Oliver, p. 130.

15. O. A. Olsen to A. T. Robinson, Oct. 25, 1892; see Knight, *Organizing*, pp. 78-80 for the sequence of events.

16. See Knight, *Organizing*, pp. 76-80.

17. Ellen G. White, MS 43a, 1901.

18. *General Conference Bulletin*, Apr. 3, 1901, p. 26; italics supplied.

19. A. G. Daniells to George LaMunyon, Oct. 7, 1901, cited in Gerry Chudleigh, *Who Runs the Church? Understanding the Unity, Structure and Authority of the Seventh-day Adventist Church* (Lincoln, NE: AdventSource, 2013), p. 18.

20. Ellen G. White, MS 26, Apr. 3, 1903; italics supplied.

21. Chudleigh, p. 18; italics supplied.

22. *Ibid.*

23. *General Conference Bulletin*, 1901, pp. 69, 464.

24. Ellen G. White, "Bring an Offering to the Lord," *Review and Herald*, Nov. 26, 1901, p. 761.

25. Ellen G. White, MS 26, Apr. 3, 1903; *General Conference Bulletin*, Apr. 25, 1901, p. 462.

26. A. G. Daniells to E. R. Palmer, Aug. 28, 1901; cited in Chudleigh, p. 16; italics supplied.

27. *General Conference Bulletin*, Mar. 31, 1903, p. 18.

28. Ellen G. White to J. Arthur, Jan. 14, 1903; italics supplied.

29. J. H. Kellogg to W. C. White, Aug. 7, 1895; C. H. Parsons to A. G. Daniells, July 6, 1903.

30. Ellen G. White, MS 26, Apr. 3, 1903.

31. Ellen G. White to A. G. Daniells and His Fellow Workers, Apr. 12, 1903.

32. See Oliver, p. 202, n. 3.

33. Ellen G. White to the General Conference Committee and the Publishing Boards of the Review and Herald and Pacific Press, Apr. 8, 1894; see also E. G. White, *Testimonies for the Church* (Mountain View, CA: Pacific Press Pub. Assn., 1948), vol. 9, pp. 259-260.

34. A. G. Daniells, *European Conference Bulletin*, p. 2, cited in Oliver, p. 320.

35. See George R. Knight, *A. T. Jones: Point Man on Adventism's Charismatic Frontier* (Hagerstown, MD: Review and Herald Pub. Assn., 2011), pp. 213-215.

36. Oliver, pp. 317 n. 2, 341.

37. *Ibid.*, pp. 346, 338, 339, 355, 345 n. 1, 340; italics supplied.

38. Chudleigh, pp. 31-37.

39. James White, "Organization," *Review and Herald*, Aug. 5, 1873, p. 60.

40. "Sixteenth Annual Session of the General Conference of S. D. Adventists," *Review and Herald*, Oct. 4, 1877, p. 106; italics supplied.

41. Ellen G. White, "Board and Council Meetings," MS 33, [no date] 1891.

42. Ellen G. White to Men Who Occupy Responsible Positions, July 1, 1896.

43. Ellen G. White, "Regarding the Southern Work," MS 37, Apr. 1901.

44. Oliver, pp. 98-99.

45. Ellen G. White, *Testimonies*, vol. 9, pp. 260-261.

46. "Sixteenth Annual Session," *Review and Herald*, Oct. 4, 1877, p. 106.

47. See *Working Policy of the General Conference of Seventh-day Adventists*, L50, L35.

48. General Conference Secretariat, "Unions and Ordination to the Gospel Ministry"; see *Working Policy* L 35 as the basis of discussion.

49. Gary Patterson, untitled critique of the Secretariat's paper on "Unions and Ordination," p. 1.

50. "Sixteenth Annual Session," *Review and Herald*, Oct. 4, 1877, p. 106.

51. James White, "Making Us a Name," *Review and Herald*, Apr. 26, 1860, p. 180; George R. Knight, "Ecclesiastical Deadlock: James White Solves a Problem that Had No Answer," *Ministry*, July 2014, pp. 9-13.

52. [Gary Patterson], "Does the General Conference Have Authority?" p. 9.

53. "Session Actions," *Adventist Review*, July 13, 1990, p. 15.

54. Ellen G. White, "Consumers, but not Producers," MS 35, 1901.

55. Ellen G. White, *The Acts of the Apostles* (Mountain View, CA: Pacific Press Pub. Assn., 1911), p. 162; see also my sermon on "The Biblical Meaning of Ordination" on YouTube and other venues.

56. Ellen G. White, *Acts of the Apostles*, pp. 161-162.

57. Russell L. Staples, "A Theological Understanding of Ordination," in Nancy Vyhmeister, ed., *Women in Ministry: Biblical and Historical Perspectives* (Berrien Springs, MI: Andrews University Press, 1998), p. 139.

58. Francis D. Nichol, ed., *The Seventh-day Adventist Bible Commentary* (Washington, DC: Review and Herald, 1953-1957), vol. 5, p. 448.

CHAPTER THREE

Catholic or Adventist: The Ongoing Struggle Over Authority + 9.5 Theses*

O n October 31, 1517, Martin Luther nailed his 95 Theses to the door of the Castle Church in Wittenberg, Germany. This year the Protestant world is celebrating the 500th anniversary of that event. On May 8 General Conference president Ted

---

* This chapter was developed as a presentation for the Unity 2017 Conference sponsored by 10 union conferences from four divisions held in London in June 2017. The stimulus for the meetings was the recommendation from the General Conference presidential offices in September 2016 to dissolve the Pacific and Columbia Union Conferences and recreate them as missions. That approach was dropped. Subsequently, the General Conference Secretariat the same month developed a 50-page document entitled "A Study of Church Governance and Unity" that highlighted the need for unity and the improper stance of those union conferences out of harmony with General Conference policy, with a focus on noncompliance over issues of ordination. This chapter is in part a critique of the positions set forth in that paper. The final outcome of the October 2016 General Conference meetings was to recommend that a procedure be developed to deal with the noncompliant unions. That procedure was to be spelled out in more detail at the October 2017 Annual Council. The Unity 2017 meetings were called to formulate a response to the actions of the General Conference.

   It should be noted that the section of this paper on "The Earliest Adventists and Ecclesiastical Authority" (pp. 80-84) and the first part of the section on "Ecclesiastical Tensions" (pp. 84-89) have borrowed heavily from material in the first two chapters.

Wilson, addressing the faculty of Middle East University, cited Ellen White, who predicted that Seventh-day Adventists would carry that Reformation on until the end of time. Beyond that, he quoted 2 Timothy 1:7: "For God has not given us a spirit of fear, but of power and of love and of a sound mind" (NKJV).[1] With that good advice in mind, we will begin our study of the history of authority in Adventism with Luther and his struggle with the Roman Church.

Given my topic, many people would expect me to deal with the theme of the development of ecclesiastical authority in Adventism. But the authority of the church in the denomination is contexted within Adventism's understanding of the authority of the Bible and that of Ellen White. As a result, I have divided this chapter into three parts: Adventism's approach to biblical authority, Ellen White's thoughts on authority, and the development of authoritative structures in the Seventh-day Adventist Church.

Adventism's Historical Approach to Biblical Authority

Adventism has historically viewed itself as a child of the Protestant Reformation. As a result, it is crucial that we recognize that the Reformation was not primarily about indulgences or even justification by faith. At its heart the Reformation was about the issue of authority.

"What is new in Luther," Heiko Oberman writes, "is the notion of absolute obedience to the Scriptures against any authorities; be they popes or councils."[2] That thought is evident in his testimony before the Diet of Worms: "Unless I am convinced by the testimony of the Holy Scriptures or by evident reason—for I can believe neither pope nor councils alone...—I consider myself convicted by the testimony of Holy Scripture, which is my basis; my conscience is captive to the Word of God. Thus I cannot and will not recant, because acting against one's conscience is neither safe nor sound. God help me. Amen."[3]

Ellen White's comments on Luther in *The Great Controversy* are helpful. Luther "firmly declared that Christians should receive no other doctrines than those which rest on the authority of the Sacred Scriptures. These words struck at the very foundation of papal supremacy. They contained the vital principle of the Reformation."[4] Again she penned, the Romanists "sought to maintain their power, not by appealing to the Scriptures, but by a resort to threats."[5] Finally, we read that "in our time there is a wide departure from their [the Scriptures'] doctrines and precepts, and there is need of a return to the great Protestant principle—the Bible, and the Bible only, as the rule of faith and duty.... The same unswerving adherence to the word of God manifested at that crisis of the Reformation is the only hope of reform today."[6]

At this point it is important to realize that Adventism's primary Reformation heritage is not Lutheranism or Calvinism but Anabaptism or the Radical Reformation, which in essence held that the magisterial reformers had not been consistent in their Bible-only approach. For the Anabaptists it was wrong to stop where Luther, Calvin, or Zwingli did theologically. As a result, they moved beyond such teachings as infant baptism and state support of the church and toward the ideals of the New Testament church.

Perhaps the best representative religious body in the spirit of Anabaptism in 19th-century America was the Restorationist movement, for which there was no creed but the Bible itself. Their drive to get back to the Bible set the stage for Adventism. Both Joseph Bates and James White came to Adventism from the Christian Connexion, a branch of Restorationism. For White, "every Christian is...in duty bound to take the Bible as a perfect rule of faith and duty."[7]

In summary, Adventism at its best in 2017 stands on a firm platform of the Bible only as the rule of faith and practice. One of the unfortunate features of Roman Catholicism and many other Christian movements in history is that when they could not establish their claims from the Bible they were tempted to use threats and force backed up by ecclesiastical authority.

At this point in our discussion of biblical authority we need to briefly examine two passages: the Jerusalem Council of Acts 15 and the binding and loosening function of the church in Matthew 18:18. Those passages have become important due to their use in recent documents produced by the General Conference. In those documents a favorite passage is Acts 15. A September 2016 document notes that "what is often called the 'Jerusalem Council' is significant almost as much for its process as for the theological decision that resulted." The decision of the Council "was regarded as binding on churches everywhere." And, we read, "in summary, the lesson of the Jerusalem Council is this: in the Church, *diversity of practice can be allowed, but only after a representative body has agreed to allow some variation.*"[8] That is an astounding conclusion, since *the lesson from the Jerusalem Council is exactly the opposite.* In Acts 15 the diversity had already been taking place. The Council met and validated that existing diversity, which previously had been blessed by the Holy Spirit.

But, as we will see, that reversal of fact is only one problematic aspect of the September 2016 document's use of Acts 15 when viewed from the perspective of what has actually taken place in recent Adventist history. But before treating that history it will be helpful to examine Ellen White's remarks on the Council. In *The Acts of the Apos-*

tles she notes that "it was the voice of the highest authority upon the earth," a descriptor she would also apply to General Conference sessions. Those words are also found in *The Story of Redemption*, where the section on the Council has the editorial title of "*The First General Conference.*" The section notes that the Council was called because the Jews did not believe that God would authorize a change from traditional practices. But, she concludes that "God Himself had decided this question by favoring the Gentiles with the Holy Ghost" to demonstrate the need for change. In short, God had given the Spirit to the Gentiles in the same manner as He had to the Jews.[9] Thus unity in diversity was approved.

The point about the Spirit settling the matter is an interesting one, since at the 2015 General Conference session there was no testimony from female pastors regarding how the Holy Spirit had blessed their ministries in the same way as that of males, the very type of testimony that had led to breaking the deadlock over accepting Gentiles in Acts 15 (see verses 8-9) and had reinforced many members of the General Conference-appointed Theology of Ordination Study Committee to approve by a strong majority the concept of allowing those divisions that desired to ordain females to move forward. In that sense the decision-making process of Acts 15 was not followed in 2015.

A further point to note is that in Acts 15 all of the decisions had a clear biblical base. The same cannot be said of the 2015 General Conference session vote, as we will see in our treatment of Adventism's ecclesiological authority.

Several other points should be made in relation to Acts 15. First, Paul later opted to not follow the Council's decision of Acts 15:20, 29 in regard to abstaining from food sacrificed to idols. That is evident from 1 Corinthians 10:23-30,[10] where in verses 25 and 27 he claims that it is permissible to eat meat offered to idols if it does not offend anyone, a ruling that goes directly against Acts 15 with its categorical prohibition. So we find Paul adding conditions and making exceptions based on cultural context. What Paul could have done was to announce that the first General Conference in session had passed a universal rule and that he had a copy of the letter to prove it. That would have solved the problem and saved Paul a lot of ink and explanation. In actuality, we do not find Paul in any of his letters referring to the Acts 15 Council, even though it could have been helpful to him.

A second point that should be noted is that the Seventh-day Adventist Church does not follow the "universal" rulings of Acts 15:20, 29 in that it does not prohibit the eating of blood by requiring flesh eaters in its midst to eat only kosher meat that has been killed in the proper way so that the blood is drained completely from it. So we find the Adventists being similar to Paul in interpreting and discarding aspects of the ruling largely based on cultural considerations.

With those facts in mind, it can be argued that the real lesson to be gained from Acts 15 is one of unity in diversity, with Jewish and Gentile Christians having freedom to follow differing paths because the Holy Spirit fell in the same way on both groups.

Regarding Matthew 18:18, the September 2016 documents produced by the General Conference Secretariat claim that "Seventh-day Adventists believe the authority granted to the Church by Jesus enables Church leaders to make decisions that bind all members." Such leadership decisions, the documents note, are made "at GC Sessions and Annual Councils."[11]

That is an interesting perspective, especially in the light of the Roman Catholic Church's usage of that passage and its parallel in

Matthew 16:19 to teach that whatever the church votes on earth is ratified in heaven. But the Greek in the verse actually says that "whatever you bind on the earth will have been bound in heaven." (cf. NASB). *The Seventh-day Adventist Bible Commentary* has it correct when it notes that "even here Heaven's ratification of the decision on earth will take place only if the decision is made in harmony with the principles of Heaven."[12]

The *Commentary*'s remark on the parallel passage in Matthew 16:19 is even clearer. Namely, the binding and loosening function of the church is "to require or to prohibit whatever Inspiration clearly reveals. But to go beyond this is to substitute human authority for the authority of Christ..., a tendency that Heaven will not tolerate in those who have been appointed to the oversight of the citizens of the kingdom of heaven on earth."[13] Ellen White makes the same point when she notes that "whatever the church does that is in accordance with the directions given in God's word will be ratified in heaven."[14]

What is most interesting in the General Conference's repeated use of the binding and loosening verses is that it consistently uses Matthew 18:18 and neglects Matthew 16:19. That is understandable since Matthew 16:18-19 not only sets forth the binding function of the church but also contains Christ's remark about Peter and the rock upon which Christ will build His church and the keys of the kingdom, making it the foundation of Roman Catholic ecclesiology. With that in mind, it is easier to see why the General Conference documents emphasize Matthew 18:18 but avoid the parallel passage. There is not much to be gained in using Catholicism's favorite passage even if it makes the same essential point. But a fascinating aspect of the use of those verses is that both the Adventists in their recent documents and the Roman Catholics have misread the text in the same manner for similar ends.

One interesting point related to the General Conference's use of Matthew 18 is that it is not the church that calls pastors but, according to Ephesians 4:11, God. All the earthly church can do is bind or ratify God's decision through commissioning or ordaining. That is biblical, as is the laying on of hands in recognition of God's call. What is not biblical is ordination as we know it. In fact, our English word "ordination" does not derive from "any Greek word used in the New Testament, but from the Latin *ordinaire*."[15] As a result, modern translations tend to use such words as "appoint" or "consecrate" where the KJV uses "ordain."[16] *The word "ordination" as Adventists use it is not a biblical teaching but one that finds its roots in the early and early-medieval church.*[17] *From that perspective, the distinction between ordaining and commissioning is a word game of no biblical substance.*

Ellen White's Historical Approach to Authority

At the very heart of Ellen White's understanding of religious authority was the place of the Bible. "The Bible," she wrote, "must be our standard for every doctrine and practice.... We are to receive no one's opinion without comparing it with the Scriptures. Here is divine authority which is supreme in matters of faith. It is the word of the living God that is to decide all controversies."[18] That thought undergirded Ellen White's theology throughout her long ministry.

In regard to her own authority, she (as did the other founders of Adventism) regarded it as derived from the authority of Scripture and subservient to it. She pictured her relation to the Bible as "a lesser light to lead men and women to the greater light."[19]

In many ways the most enlightening episode regarding Ellen White's position on authority took place in relation to the 1888 General Conference session.[20] At that event she had to confront those pushing traditional Adventist perspectives at several levels of human authority. One approach was General Conference president G. I. Butler's self-perception of having "the highest position that our people could impose" and his claim of special rights and responsibilities in settling theological issues in the church. Ellen White made short shrift of that approach. Soon after the 1888 meetings she wrote that Butler "thinks his position gives him such power that his voice is infallible." "No man is to be authority for us," she penned.[21]

A second approach she had to deal with was the attempt to use Adventist tradition to solve the biblical issues. She responded to that tactic by writing that "as a people we are certainly in great danger, if we are not constantly guarded, of considering our ideas, because long cherished, to be Bible doctrines and on every point infallible, and measuring everyone by the rule of our interpretation of Bible truth. This is our danger, and this would be the greatest evil that could ever come to us as a people."[22]

A third category of human authority she had to face in the 1888 era was the drive at the Minneapolis session to solve the theological and biblical issues by establishing the denomination's official position through a formal vote of the General Conference in session. As usual, Ellen White had words for the denomination on that topic. "*The church*," she penned, "*may pass resolution upon resolution to put down all disagreement of opinions, but we cannot force the mind and will, and thus root out disagreement. These resolutions may conceal the discord, but they cannot quench it and establish perfect agreement. Nothing can perfect unity in the church but the spirit of Christlike forbearance.*" W. C. White expressed his view regarding an official vote to settle the disputed issues by declaring to the Minneapolis delegates that he would feel compelled "to preach what he believed, whatever way the conference decided the question" at hand.[23]

Unrelated to the 1888 event, but intimately connected to the problem of churchly authority, is Ellen White's statement in *The Great Controversy* that *"the very beginning of the great apostasy was in seeking to supplement the authority of God by that of the church."*[24]

A second major topic related to Ellen White's historic view on authority has to do with the General Conference as God's highest authority on earth. That topic will be treated in the next major section of this chapter, which deals with ecclesiastical authority in Adventism.

But before moving to that topic we need to examine briefly Ellen White's perspective on ordination. We noted earlier that ordination as practiced by the church is not a biblical issue. But, according to Ellen White, it did become an important issue in the history of the early church. In treating the laying of hands on Paul and Barnabas in Acts 13:3, she writes that God "instructed the church...to set them apart publicly to the work of the ministry. Their *ordination was a public recognition of their divine appointment.*" They *"had already received their commission from God Himself,* and *the ceremony* of the laying on of hands *added no new grace or virtual qualification....* By it the seal of the church was set upon the work of God.... *At a later date the rite of ordination by the laying on of hands was greatly abused; unwarrantable importance was attached to the act,* as if a power came at once upon those who received such ordination."[25] In speaking of the same event in another place she says much the same thing, but adds that their ordination by the laying on of hands "was merely setting the seal of the church upon the work of God—an acknowledged form of designation to an appointed office."[26]

By speaking of abuse of the term "ordination" in the church, Ellen White is undoubtedly referring in part to the sacerdotal approach to the authority of the priesthood conferred by ordination that gave them such power as to transform the bread and wine into the actual body and blood of Christ. But more to the point is the hierarchical power of the higher clergy, in which excessive authority has traditionally been granted to bishops with special headship function as fathers of the church. Such power is conferred through the "sacrament of holy orders or ordination."[27]

Given the amount of heat generated in some Adventist circles on the topic of ordination, one might surmise that somehow power and authority is being transferred to the ordinand. While that might do for Roman Catholic theology, it does not hold up in either the Bible or Ellen White. To the contrary, just as baptism does not erase original sin but is rather an outward symbol of a changed heart, and just as the bread and the wine are not magically transformed into the actual body and blood of Christ in the sacrifice of the Mass but are rather symbols of what Christ accomplished on the cross, so it is that the laying on of hands in what has come to be called ordination does not confer power but is symbolic in recognition of the power already conferred by God in the calling and empowerment of a pastor. *What counts is not the act of ordination but the calling of God.* And the Seventh-day Adventist Church has for many years recognized that God calls both men and women to pastoral ministry. The only difference is that the church has opted to call one ordination and the other commissioning. Such non-biblical verbal gymnastics must lead the angels to scratch their heads in bewilderment. However, it all seems to be clear in Adventist policy.

But at least Ellen White is forthright on the topic. No power or authority is transferred in ordination. That is a product of the history of the church. And, in the words of the Revelator, much of the Christian world seems to be following after the beast (Revelation 13:3, NKJV) on the understanding and importance of ordination.

Historical Issues in Adventism's Approach to Ecclesiology

So far this paper has examined Adventism's approach to biblical authority and Ellen White's historical approach to authority. Thus the stage has been set for an examination of the denomination's struggle to find and be faithful to a balanced and biblical view of ecclesiastical authority.

The Earliest Adventists and Ecclesiastical Authority: 1843-1863

Looking back at early Adventism, no one could have predicted that by mid-20th century Seventh-day Adventism would be the most highly structured denomination in the history of Christianity, with four levels of authority above the local congregation.[28] The plain fact is that the earliest Adventists feared structured churches. And with good reason. That fear is nicely expressed in the October 1861 meeting that saw the establishment of the first local conference. Part of the discussion at that historic meeting had to do with developing a formal statement of belief. John Loughborough took the lead in the discussion and laid out five progressive points that nicely express the attitude of most of his audience.

- "The first step of apostasy," he noted, "is to get up a creed, telling us what we shall believe.
- "The second is, to make that creed a test of fellowship.
- "The third is to try members by that creed.

- "The fourth to denounce as heretics those who do not believe that creed.
- "And, fifth, to commence persecution against such."[29]

James White also expressed his fears. "Making a creed," he declared, "is setting the stakes, and barring up the way to all future advancement." Those churches that had set up creeds "have marked out a course for the Almighty. They say virtually that the Lord must not do anything further than what has been marked out in the creed.... The Bible is our creed. We reject everything in the form of a human creed. We take the Bible and the gifts of the Spirit; embracing the faith that thus the Lord will teach us from time to time. And in this we take a position against the formation of a creed. We are not taking one step, in what we are doing, toward becoming Babylon [as oppression]."[30]

Those points are informative to those of us who live 150 years later. While White feared a backward looking rigidity that would inhibit the progressive dynamic in what the early Adventists thought of as an ongoing present truth, Loughborough expressed fear of persecution for those who did not line up with official positions.

And the participants in that 1861 meeting had good reasons to fear organized religious bodies. Fresh in their memories was the persecution of Millerites in 1843 and 1844 as pastors lost their pulpits and followers their memberships because of their belief in the Bible's teaching on the Second Advent. They had come to see organized religion in terms of the persecuting Babylon of the books of Daniel and Revelation. It was no accident that Millerite George Storrs wrote in early 1844 that "no church can be organized by man's invention but what it becomes Babylon *the moment it is organized*." In the same article Storrs asserted that Babylon "is the *old mother* and all her children [the Protestant denominations]; who are known by the family like-ness, a domineering, lordly spirit; a spirit to suppress a free search after truth, and a free expression of our conviction of what is truth."[31] Charles Fitch had been of the same opinion in his famous sermon calling Millerites to come out of Babylon, the fallen denominations.[32]

It was the fear of Babylon as persecuting churches that kept any of the six major groups that came out of the Millerite movement from organizing before the 1850s and 1860s. And none but the Sabbatar-ian Adventists would ever organize above the congregational level.[33]

The fear of organized denominations as persecuting Babylon stands at the foundation of early Adventist attitudes in regard to or-ganizing as a church. But in the 1850s James White began to empha-size an alternate biblical meaning of Babylon. In July 1859 he let it be known in the most descriptive language that he was sick and tired of the cry of Babylon every time that anyone mentioned organiza-tion. "Bro. Confusion," he penned, "makes a most egregious blunder in calling system, which is in harmony with the Bible and good sense, Babylon. As Babylon signifies confusion, our erring brother has the very word stamped upon his own forehead. And we venture to say that there is not another people under heaven more worthy of the brand of Babylon than those professing the Advent faith who reject Bible order. Is it not high time that we as a people heartily embrace everything that is good and right in the churches?"[34]

It is impossible to overestimate the force of White's redirection of the emphasis from Babylon being primarily seen as persecution to that of confusion. That new emphasis went far toward paving the way for the Sabbatarians to organize as a religious body, legally own property, pay pastors on a regular basis, assign pastors to locations where they were needed, and develop a system for transferring membership. In the end, developing church organization had one major end: namely, to expedite the mission of the denomination.

But the redefinition of Babylon was only one of the transformations that allowed the Sabbatarian Adventists to organize. A second essential transformation had to do with moving beyond the biblical literalism of White's earlier days when he believed that the Bible must explicitly spell out each aspect of church organization. In 1859 he argued that "we should not be afraid of that system which is not opposed by the Bible, and is approved by sound sense."[35] *Thus he had come to a new hermeneutic. White had moved from a principle of Bible interpretation that held that the only things Scripture allowed were those things it explicitly approved to a hermeneutic that allowed for developments that did not contradict the Bible and were in harmony with common sense. That shift was absolutely essential to moving forward in the creative steps in church organization that he would advocate in the 1860s.*

That revised hermeneutic, however, put White in opposition to those who maintained a literalistic approach to the Bible that demanded that it explicitly spell something out before the church could accept it. To answer that mentality, White noted that nowhere in the Bible did it say that Christians should have a weekly paper, operate a steam printing press, build places of worship, or publish books. He went on to argue that the "living church of God" needed to move forward with prayer and common sense.[36]

Without the radical shift in hermeneutical principles there would have been no organization among the Sabbatarians above the local congregation. But the new hermeneutic allowed them not only to organize but to create a structure that made it possible to take their unique message to the ends of the earth. Mission, we must note again, was always behind the Adventist mentality as it sought to dynamically move forward on the basis of a hermeneutic that allowed those things that did not contradict the Bible and were in harmony with common sense.

With the new hermeneutic and the new definition of Babylon in place, the Sabbatarians were in position to develop the non-biblical concept of local conferences in 1861 and the equally non-biblical concept of a General Conference in 1863. That last move was "for the purpose of securing unity and efficiency in labor, and promoting the general interests of the cause of present truth, and of perfecting the organization of the Seventh-day Adventists."[37]

Ecclesiastical Tensions and the Creation of Unions: 1863-1903

As might be expected, tensions eventually developed between the authority of the local conferences and that of the General Conference. In August 1873, for example, in the context of a lack of respect for General Conference officers, James White noted that "our General Conference is the highest earthly authority with our people, and is designed to take charge of the entire work in this and all other countries."[38]

Then in 1877 the General Conference in session voted that "the highest authority under God among Seventh-day Adventists is found in the will of the body of that people, as expressed in the decisions of the General Conference *when acting within its proper jurisdiction*; and that such decisions should be submitted to by all without exception, *unless they can be shown to conflict with the word of God and the rights of individual conscience.*"[39]

That vote seems clear enough and both of the Whites accepted it. Please note, however, that it did highlight limitations related to the "proper jurisdiction" of the General Conference and "the rights of individual conscience."

Interestingly, Ellen White on several occasions questioned whether the rulings of the General Conference were always the voice of God. In 1891, for example, she wrote that "I was obliged to take the position that there was not the voice of God in the General Conference management and decisions.... Many of the positions taken, going forth as the voice of the General Conference, have been the voice of one, two, or three men who were misleading the Conference."[40] Again in 1896 she noted that the General Conference "is no longer the voice of God."[41] And in 1901 she wrote that "the people have lost confidence in those who have management of the work. Yet we hear that the voice of the [General] Conference is the voice of God. Every time I have heard this, I have thought that it was almost blasphemy. The voice of the conference ought to be the voice of God, but it is not."[42]

An analysis of those negative statements indicates that they refer to occasions when the General Conference did not act as a representative body, when its decision-making authority was centralized in a person or a few people, or when the General Conference had not been following sound principles.[43]

That conclusion lines up with Ellen White's statements across time. In fact, she specifically spoke to the point in a manuscript read before the delegates of the 1909 General Conference session in which she responded to the schismatic activities of A. T. Jones and others. "At times," she told the delegates, "when a small group of men entrusted with the general management of the work have, in the name of the General Conference, sought to carry out unwise plans and to restrict God's work, I have said that I could no longer regard the voice of the General Conference, represented by these few men, as the voice of God. But this is not saying that the decisions of a General Conference composed of an assembly of duly appointed, representative men from all parts of the field should not be respected. God has ordained that the representatives of His church from all parts of the earth, when assembled in a General Conference, shall have authority."[44]

The second round of organizational refinement took place between 1901 and 1903,[45] when several major changes were made. The two most important were the replacement of the autonomous auxiliary organizations (such as those that controlled education, publishing, medical, Sabbath school, and so on) with the departmental system and the development of union conferences to stand as intermediary administrative units between the General Conference and the local conferences. Both of those innovations had been experimented with in South Africa and Australia before the 1901 session. Both of them had been developed in response to regional mission needs. And both were developed in opposition to General Conference pronouncements and procedures.

General Conference president O. A. Olsen thought he saw "elements of danger" in the departmental system and told A. T. Robinson in South Africa not to develop departments.[46] But it was too late. Because of the large amount of time it took to communicate from North America, Robinson had instituted the program and found out that it worked.

It is of interest that the General Conference leadership also opposed the creation of union conferences.[47] But W. C. White and A. G. Daniells, president and secretary of the Australian field, moved forward in spite of counsel from headquarters. Years later Daniells reported that not everyone was happy with the union conference idea. "Some of our brethren thought then that the work was going to be wrecked, that we were going to tear the organization all to pieces, and get up secession out there in the South Sea islands." But in actuality, he observed, the result was quite the opposite. The new organizational approach greatly facilitated the mission of the church in the South Pacific while the new Australasian Union Conference remained a loyal and integral part of the General Conference system.[48]

Here we need to remember an important lesson in the history of Adventist organization. Namely, that both of the major innovations adopted by the 1901 General Conference session were in response to regional mission and both were developed in opposition to General Conference counsel. But they worked. The major lesson is that without the freedom to experiment Adventism would not have its present system of organization.

Ellen White was overjoyed with the development of union conferences. In calling for reform on the first day of the 1901 session she noted to the delegates that "God has not put any kingly power in our ranks to control this or that branch of the work. The work has been greatly restricted by the efforts to control it in every line.... If the work had not been so restricted by an impediment here, and an impediment there, and on the other side an impediment, it would have gone forward in its majesty."[49] At the 1903 session she declared that *"it has been a necessity to organize Union conferences, that the General Conference shall not exercise dictation over all the separate Conferences."*[50]

On the basis of those and other comments, the late Gerry Chudleigh has argued that the unions "were created to act as *firewalls* between the GC and the conferences, making 'dictation' impossible." He buttressed his firewall image with two major points. First, "each union had its own constitution and bylaws and was to be governed by its own constituency." And, second, "the officers of each union were to be elected by their own union constituency, and, therefore, could not be controlled, replaced or disciplined by the GC."[51]

"To put it as bluntly as possible," Chudleigh wrote, "after 1901, the General Conference could vote whatever it wanted unions and conferences to do, or not do, but the unions and conferences were autonomous and could do what they believed would best advance the work of God in their fields. The GC executive committee, or the General Conference in business session, could vote to fire a union president or conference president, or vote to merge a union or conference with another one, but their vote would change nothing: the union or conference would still exist and the member delegates could elect whoever they wanted as president."[52] A case in point in contemporary Adventism is the Southeastern California Conference, which has an ordained female president, in spite of the wishes of the General Conference.

The situation looked good in 1901 with the union conferences in place. But the push for both unity and uniformity by the General Conference over time would erode the accomplishments of 1901. The most significant move along that line, as we will see, took place at the 1995 General Conference session.

The erosion of the ideal of unity in diversity had, unfortunately, already begun soon after the 1901 session. The following two years would witness a major struggle for the control of Adventism between General Conference president A. G. Daniells and J. H. Kellogg, the powerful leader of the denomination's medical work.

Ellen White back in 1894 had set forth "unity in diversity" as

"God's plan," with unity being achieved by each aspect of the work being connected to Christ the vine.[53] In 1901 and 1902 Daniells had championed that ideal, noting in 1902 to the European Union Conference that just "because a thing is done a certain way in one place is not reason why it should be done in the same way in another place, or even in the same place at the same time."[54]

But that ideal began to give way by late 1902 as the Kellogg forces sought to unseat Daniells and replace him with A. T. Jones, who was by that time in the doctor's camp. In that struggle the Kellogg/Jones forces pushed for diversity. That dynamic impelled Daniells to emphasize unity as he moved toward a more authoritative stance. Thus the delicate balance related to unity in diversity lost out soon after the 1901 session. And, as Barry Oliver points out, unity at the expense of diversity has been the focus of the General Conference leadership ever since the 1902 crisis.[55]

The only significant development in Adventist church structure since 1901/1903 took place in 1918 with the creation of world divisions of the General Conference. But it should be noted that the divisions are not conferences with their own constituencies but parts of the General Conference administration that represent the central body in various parts of the world.[56]

An ongoing temptation of the General Conference throughout its history has been to overstep the bounds of its authority. General Conference president George I. Butler generated one of the boldest moves in that direction in 1873. "Never," he penned on the first page of his little book titled *Leadership*, was there a "great movement in this world without a leader.... As nature bestows upon men a variety of gifts, it follows that some have clearer views than others of what best advances the interests of any cause. And the best good of all interested in any given object will be attained by intelligently following the counsels of those best qualified to guide." Butler had no doubt that James White had played a role akin to that of Moses, and that in all matters of expediency in the Adventist cause it was right "to give his [White's] judgment the preference."[57] The 1873 General Conference session officially adopted Butler's ideas. But both of the Whites eventually felt uncomfortable with the document and wrote against many of its principles.[58] As a result, the 1875 and 1877 sessions rescinded the endorsement, especially those sections dealing with leadership being "confined to any one man."[59]

Kevin Burton in his recent MA thesis on Butler's *Leadership* did an excellent job of demonstrating that Butler wrote with James White as the leader he had in mind. But the self-imposed scope of Burton's research did not allow for the demonstration that Butler's style and claims in the 1873 document mirror his own style and claims in the 1888 conflict.[60] On October 1, 1888, Butler wrote a long letter to Ellen White repeatedly emphasizing that he had "the highest position" in the denomination and should have the rights that go with that position. She replied to him on October 14 that he did "not understand [his] true position," that he had "false ideas of what belonged to [his] position," that he had turned his "mind into wrong channels," that he had "not kept pace with the opening providence of God," and that he had mingled his "natural traits of character" with his work. *Most serious of all the charges was that he was seeking to manipulate the information that would come before the 1888 General Conference session.* Speaking to the General Conference president and Uriah Smith (the secretary), she wrote that "you must not think that the Lord has placed you in the position that you now occupy as the only men who are to decide as to whether any more light and truth shall come to

God's people." She noted in this letter and others that Butler's influence had led other session delegates to also "disregard light."[61]

A broad study of the 1888 crisis indicates that the most serious problem troubling the Minneapolis meeting was the high-handed assertions of position and manipulation of data by the president and his colleagues.[62] It should be noted in passing that the theme of Butler's 1873 *Leadership* was "union" and "order."[63] Unity was the goal in that document and the same preservation of unity would be Butler's goal in the manipulation of data in the 1888 period.

Butler, as we know, lost the 1888 struggle. He had sought to impose not only unity but theological uniformity on the denomination. But Ellen White pushed against him with the alternate ideal of unity in diversity. She was, the General Conference's newly elected secretary reported in 1890, not so much interested in theological unity as she was in the unity of having a Christ-like spirit built on brotherly love.[64]

The major lesson to flow out of the 1888 crisis is unity in diversity. That same principle would undergird the reform of church structures in 1901. As we saw earlier, the unity in diversity ideal had begun to run into major difficulties in 1902 when Daniells began to assert his authority as General Conference president in his struggle with Kellogg. At that point, diversity began to take a back seat to unity and Ellen White in 1903 had to warn the reforming General Conference president that he could not "exercise a kingly power over [his] brethren."[65]

Removal of the Union Conference Firewall: 1980-2016

In spite of Daniells' temptation to wrongly use the power of his office, the balance between unity and diversity institutionalized by the creation of union conferences fared tolerably well for most of the 20th century. In his summary of that period, Gerry Chudleigh notes that the constitutions and bylaws created and voted at the 1901 session for the first unions "contained no requirement that the unions adopt or follow GC policies, procedures, programs, initiatives, etc."[66]

But that would begin to change in the legal documents of the denomination in the 1980s and come to a climax in the 1990s and the first two decades of the 21st century. The 1980s witnessed the development by the General Conference of a "Model Union Conference Constitution and Bylaws." In 1985 the *Working Policy* stated that the model should be "followed as closely as possible." But by 1995 the same section would note that the model "shall be followed by all union conferences.... Those sections of the model bylaws that appear in bold print are essential to the unity of the Church worldwide, and shall be included in the bylaws as adopted by each union conference. Other sections of the model may be modified." In 1985 the model stipulated that all **"purposes and procedures"** of the unions would be in harmony with the **"working policies and procedures"** of the General Conference. By 1995 General Conference **"programs and initiatives"** had been added. And in 2000 all **"policies"** was included. All of those additions were in bold print.[67] Thus between 1985 and 2000 the *Working Policy* not only erased the 1901 model of unity in diversity set forth for unions in the Ellen White led drive for decentralization, but had become progressively more engineered toward centralization of authority in a drive for unity with less and less diversity.

The challenge for the General Conference in the mid-'80s was to get existing union conferences to adopt the new model. In that, they succeeded in some unions and failed in others.

The case of the North Pacific Union opens a window into the dynamics. In September 1986 it rejected the model. But perhaps the most significant event connected to that rejection was the reading of General Conference president Neal Wilson's letter to the delegates. Wilson made it clear that the General Conference was the "highest authority in the church" and that it had the authority to create subordinate organizations. He then chastised the North Pacific Union for having two years before created its own constitution that was not in harmony with the model. He also threatened the noncompliant union, claiming that he saw "the only other option" to be an investigation "to determine whether [the] union...is operating within the spirit and guidelines established for union conferences, with the understanding that appropriate action will be taken in the case of organizations that do not measure up to the standard."[68]

That unvarnished threat indicates that the type of actions threatened by the General Conference in 2016 have a history. And that history is solidly rooted in the tightening up of the relationship between union conferences and the General Conference in the modified *Working Policy*.

The 1990s would witness the General Conference leadership's plan to centralize its authority move into high gear. Robert Folkenberg, the new General Conference president, faced with the important but daunting task of maintaining order in a massive world church, established in 1991 the Commission on World Church Organization, which met several times until its work was completed in 1994. The successful aspects of the Commission's work went to the 1995 General Conference session. Others fell by the wayside. All of them were aimed at the centralization of authority.

Among those that fell by the wayside was an attempt to take away the exclusive right of local congregations to disfellowship members. The stimulus for the move was the fact that Des Ford of Glacier View fame and John Osborne of Prophecy Countdown still held church membership in sympathetic congregations that would not disfellowship them. Osborne's case is interesting since, although he lived in Florida, his membership, being threatened there, had been rescued by the Troy, Montana, church where he had never lived. At that point those in the General Conference who wanted action threatened to disband the church. I still remember getting a late evening phone call from one of the congregation's leaders telling me that they had been given an ultimatum: either disfellowship Osborne or face dissolution as an Adventist church. The congregation was disbanded, but Osborne's membership had been rescued by the Village Church in Angwin, California. Interestingly enough, it was the Pacific Union College Church in the same city that held Ford's membership. Neither congregation responded to the call to disfellowship the men. But the solution seemed obvious—give higher levels of the church structure the prerogative of disfellowshipping local church members.[69] Ideally, the idea ran, the same sort of logic could be used to remove ministerial credentials and disband congregations. Thus the "higher" levels would have more control over situations that they believed the lower levels were not handling correctly.

Bert Haloviak, General Conference archivist at the time, notes that he, Paul Gordon of the White Estate, and a member of the Biblical Research Institute were summoned to Folkenberg's office and each asked to write a paper with the "hidden agenda" of supporting some of the General Conference's initiatives. The Institute's paper was written by Raoul Dederen of Andrews University. All three papers, although written independently and from different perspectives, concluded that the General Conference did not have grounding to do such things as disfellowshipping members. I recall Dederen, a colleague of mine at the time with specialties in ecclesiology and Roman Catholic theology, having remarked at the Cohutta Springs meeting of March 1993 that some of the proposed initiatives were in essence the revival of medieval Catholicism.[70]

The most successful aspects of the Commission's recommendations saw passage at the 1995 General Conference session. That session not only witnessed a further tightening of the control measures embedded in the model constitutions, but also passed legislation that allowed for noncompliant unions, conferences, and missions to be disbanded if they did not come into line with General Conference policies and initiatives. Since 1995 the *General Conference Working Policy* has contained a new section titled "Discontinuation of Conferences, Missions, Unions, and Unions of Churches by Dissolution and/or Expulsion."[71] Utilizing the ever-more centralizing requirements of the model constitution, the new section (B 95) proclaims the power to disband any union, conference, or mission that is out of harmony with General Conference policy. With what has become policy B 95 in place, the General Conference had arrived at the point where it could threaten the existence of two North American Division unions in September and October 2016.

Meanwhile, the measures attempted in the early '90s had met a fair amount of resistance both in committees and at Annual Council meetings. Susan Sickler, a member of the Governance Commission, saw it as a "huge power grab," while Herman Bauman, Arizona Conference president, said that the essence of the commission report could be spelled "with the letters C-O-N-T-R-O-L." One General Conference staffer quipped in a private conversation, "What the Catholic

Church took 300 years to achieve, we are doing in 150."[72]

Folkenberg, on the other hand, "kept saying this was in no way a centralization of power." In response, one NAD union president noted to the Commission that "if it walks like a duck and it quacks like a duck, it probably is a duck." Neal Wilson, who had his own issues with his successor, aggressively supported those who saw the issue as centralization.[73]

Ted Wilson, then president of the division encompassing Russia, was reported to have said at a commission meeting that he would have difficulty getting some of the recommendations accepted in a country that had just exited communism.[74] That, needless to say, was a pertinent insight that might have meaning in 2017 for those who understand the significance of the Protestant Reformation.

One final point needs to be made in regard to the Governance Commission. Namely, that some person or persons "high up" in the General Conference apparently manipulated the data so that the final form of the commission report did not line up with what was voted. Folkenberg did not indicate "how and why it came into final form without discussion and a vote from the commission."[75] The manipulation of data would reappear in 2015.

We now move to the 2015 General Conference session as a final building block that led up to the noncompliance threat issued at the 2016 Annual Council. The major event of the 2015 session, of course, was the vote to not allow divisions the option of ordaining female pastors. That action is clear enough. But the way it took place leaves open the question of whether the action represents a "voice of God" vote enacted by the General Conference in session.

To grasp the significance of that issue we need to go to the early presidency of Ted Wilson when he established the Theology of Ordination Study Committee (TOSC). This worldwide panel of over 100 scholars and non-scholars who had a burden on the topic met in 2013 and 2014 with the aim of informing the church on ordination issues at a scholarly level so that an informed vote could take place in 2015.[76] The study cost the denomination hundreds of thousands of dollars. As the General Conference Secretariat noted, "voices from around the world and from all sides were heard; the arguments and supporting documents of all perspectives were made freely available online.... The process was unmatched in both breadth and depth."[77] All those points are true and were included in a document that suggested penalties for those unions that had not come into line with the 2015 vote. All of this is forcefully outlined in a document entitled "A Study of Church Governance and Unity" developed by the General Conference Secretariat in September 2016.

But, unfortunately, the "Study" in actuality set the stage for disunity in that it inflated the document's value for its own purposes but did not report the findings of TOSC. That maneuver is merely the tip of a nasty iceberg.

As impossible as it seems after having spent so much money and time on the project, the results of TOSC were never clearly presented to the General Conference session at the time of the vote. And for good reason. Apparently, TOSC's consensus did not support the desired conclusions of certain individuals at the top of the denominational power structure.[78] Thus the 2015 delegates were not informed that a super majority of 2/3 (62 for and 32 opposed) of the members of TOSC was in favor of allowing divisions to make the choice on whether to ordain female pastors.[79] In addition, the delegates were not informed that at least nine[80] of the 13 divisions of the church in their TOSC reports were favorable toward letting each division make its own decision on female ordination. Nor did the final TOSC report present that data. It did, however, present the positions of three distinct groupings of delegates that developed during TOSC's two-year journey. But the delegates at the 2015 session were not explicitly informed that two of those orientations were in favor of each division making its own choice.[81]

Had the actual findings of TOSC been reported, the vote, in all probability, would have been different. After all, a 10% shift in the vote would have changed the outcome. The final tally at the General Conference session in San Antonio was 977 (42%) in favor of flexibility in ordination to 1,381 against, a remarkably close vote considering how the process was handled.

Not the least of the problems associated with the vote was the non-neutrality of the General Conference president, who reminded the session delegates on voting day that they knew his position on the topic (which was clearly understood to be against the ordination of women). That non-neutrality was bad enough, but it was stated with the full knowledge that a significant majority of TOSC, a committee that he had authorized to solve the problem, had concluded to recommend that divisions should have the right to ordain females if they chose to do so.[82] And in a world church in which the vast majority of the delegates come from tribal and Roman Catholic cultures, a word from the denomination's top administrator has significance. The Norwegian Union Conference made an important point when it suggested that if unity was high on the agenda of the General Conference president he could have clearly reported the findings of TOSC and called for a solution in line with its results.[83]

At this point the widespread "disgust" expressed by a significant number of the TOSC membership at the reversal of the General Conference president should be noted for the record. At the beginning of the meetings, when it apparently looked like the carefully selected participants would come up with the "correct" conclusion, he spoke to the committee on the importance of their work, that it was not merely another investigation into a much studied topic, but that their findings would make a difference. But when the majority recommendation went the other way, he intimated at the final meeting that it was largely a North American committee and that if it had been a world committee the decision would have been different. He was reminded publicly that although many of the members were working in North America, they were in fact from around the world. But to no avail. The findings of the committee seem at that point to have become not so important and were marginalized at the 2015 session.[84]

There were also serious irregularities in the 2015 voting, but this is not the place to discuss them.[85] On the other hand, it should be pointed out that no matter how the vote turned out or how it could have turned out, the procedure itself suffered from the suppression and manipulation of data. This is a serious charge to make, but there is no alternative in the face of the handling of the TOSC findings and the ongoing misuse of them in General Conference documents, which trumpet the importance of the study without reporting its results.[86]

William Johnsson, retired editor of the *Adventist Review*, has pointed out that 2015 will go down in history as the most divisive General Conference session since 1888.[87] And he is correct. What is interesting is that in both sessions, top people in the General Conference manipulated data. In the 1888 era it was president G. I. Butler, who Ellen White faulted for his desire to decide what information came to the delegates.[88] One can only guess who decided to suppress and manipulate the reporting of the findings of TOSC in 2015, but the only possibility is a few people near the top of the General Conference structure.

The significance of the manipulation and suppression of crucial data that had been produced at immense expense for the purpose of informing the church has vast implications, especially since Ellen White, as we saw earlier, repeatedly claimed in the 1890s that she no longer held that the General Conference was the voice of God because its decisions were really the decisions of a few men. That is exactly what we find in the events leading up to the vote in San Antonio. A few people decided what information went to the delegates. Even the General Conference's "Study of Church Governance and Unity" document pointed out that Ellen White was upset when "'two or three men'" tried to control the church's mission or when "'merely a half a dozen' at the world headquarters" sought "'to be a ruling and controlling power.'" The "Study" document was correct in its use of that inspired material. But it was dead wrong when it claimed that what happened in the late 1800s "is a world away from the situation today."[89] It was actually the same situation and dynamic, with a few people in their decision-making capacity controlling information and events. As a result, from the perspective of Ellen White's writings, we do not have a voice of God vote from the world church in 2015. Instead, we have the same old manipulation and kingly power approaches that she detested in 1888 and the 1890s.

And the manipulation was not merely of data but also of process. Here one example must suffice. The General Conference documents uplift the Acts 15 conference "almost as much for its *process* as for the theological decision that resulted," but that appreciation was not evident in San Antonio. For one thing, the General Conference documents do not describe the Acts 15 process. Rather, they infer that the process was voting, followed by mandatory obedience.[90] But Acts 15 outlines not only the actual process but also the essential tipping point in that process. The breakthrough in Acts 15 truly was based on process and came when Peter was able to demonstrate that the Holy Spirit made no distinction between Jews and Gentiles but came in the same way to both groups (Acts 15:8-9). Without that evidence there would have been nothing but ongoing divisiveness. But with it there was healing and unity. What would have happened in San Antonio if the process utilized in Acts 15 had been used on the day of the vote? There would have been testimonies from people put on the program that demonstrated that the Holy Spirit fell upon the pastoral/evangelistic ministries of women in the same way as for men. Such testimonies were important in the final TOSC meeting and helped lead to a significant majority of the participants, despite their personal position on women's ordination, to approve flexibility in the practice of ordaining women.[91] But the few people who set up the procedure in San Antonio chose not to follow the Acts 15 model, even though the "Study of Church Governance" documents cite that passage to bolster the General Conference's authoritative position.

Much more could be said about the manipulation of data and process in the events related to the 2015 vote. But the illustrations are many and my time is short. The final conclusion is that the vote settled nothing. But it did divide the denomination in ways that are tragic. Here some wisdom from James and Ellen White would have helped. James had written in 1874 that "creed power has been called to the rescue [of church unity] in vain. It has been truly said that 'The American people are a nation of lords.' In a land of boasted freedom of thought and of conscience, like ours, *church force cannot produce* unity; *but has caused divisions*, and has given rise to religious sects and parties almost innumerable."[92]

His wife was of the same opinion. "The church may pass resolution upon resolution to put down all disagreement of opinions," she penned in 1892, "but we cannot force the mind and will, and thus root out disagreement. These resolutions may conceal the discord, but they cannot quench it and establish perfect agreement."[93] From her perspective, only the clear word of Scripture could bring true unity.

Christ made a pertinent point when He proclaimed that he who has ears needs to "hear what the Spirit says to the churches" (Revelation 3:22, RSV). I once heard a very wise man say that those who like to quote Ellen White should listen to all she has to say and not just use her to get across their own goals. Here are two selections that have been relevant throughout Adventism's ongoing struggle over authority. In 1895 she penned that *"the high-handed power that has been developed, as though position has made men gods, makes me afraid,* and ought to cause fear. *It is a curse* wherever and by whomsoever it is exercised. *This lording it over God's heritage will create such a disgust of man's jurisdiction that a state of insubordination will result."* She went on to recommend that the "only safe course is to remove" such leaders since "all ye are brethren," lest "great harm be done."[94]

Another fascinating insight comes from the *Testimonies*. "One man's mind and judgment are not to be considered capable of controlling and molding a conference.... The president of a conference must not consider that his individual judgment is to control the judgment of all.... *Many, very many matters have been taken up and carried by vote, that have involved far more than was anticipated and far more than those who voted would have been willing to assent to had they* taken time to consider the question from all sides."[95] In that quotation we find some excellent advice for Adventist decision makers as they approach the 2017 Annual Council.

So Where Are We in 2017?

Since the problem that has developed in the past few years is over women's ordination, I should briefly comment on the topic.

- It is not prohibited in the Bible.
- It is not prohibited in Ellen White's writings.
- The General Conference *Working Policy* does not stipulate a gender requirement.[96]
- It is not a settled issue because of the suppression of information and the manipulation of the process in 2015.
- Its practice will not stop because there is no biblical evidence for doing so.
- Its prohibition cannot be settled by a vote alone. Adventist leaders need to refrain from seeking to use policy as if it were Catholicism's Canon Law. We need to remember that Adventism is post-Reformation.

It is true that in 1990 the denomination officially voted not to ordain women to the gospel ministry because of "the possible risk of disunity, dissension, and diversion from the mission of the church."[97] That vote, we should note, did not claim that the practice was wrong. It was not a theological vote, but one based on the practical ground that it might cause disunity. That was 27 years ago, and the denomination has discovered that unity can be fractured in more than one direction. The plain fact in 2017 is that the church is seriously divided on women's ordination. But it probably would not be if the conclusions generated by the TOSC committee had not been suppressed at San Antonio, if the process in Acts 15 had been utilized at the session, and if the General Conference leadership would have used the findings of TOSC as a tool to bring unity and healing to the church.

But that healing approach did not take place. As a result, a small group at denominational headquarters decided to exert what it believed to be its authority in September and October 2016, months that witnessed the apex of the evolution of Adventist ecclesiological authority and the continuation of the problematic results that both James and Ellen White had predicted from the use of such authority. The initial September recommendation, formulated in the presidential offices, utilized the *Working Policy* rulings developed in the 1980s and 1990s to centralize authority. Especially important was B 95, voted into policy at the 1995 session, which authorized the "dissolution" of noncompliant union conferences that were not in harmony with General Conference policy. That initial document, whose basic content was leaked to *Spectrum*, urged the disbanding of the offending unions and reconstituting them as missions attached to the General Conference. That way the union leaders could be removed and replaced and constituency meetings could be called to reverse the ordination votes.[98] My sources, many of whom requested confidentiality in the present intimidating and threatening denominational climate,[99] tell me that the initial proposal, which did not have widespread input, was withdrawn and all copies were collected by the General Conference president.

What eventually came out of a complex process was the document generated by the Secretariat titled "A Study of Church Governance and Unity." This is not the place to critique that document,[100] but its existence points to an interesting paradox. Namely, that the move by General Conference headquarters in Silver Spring to correct the noncompliant unions is out of harmony with the General Conference's own policy. Mitchell Tyner, retired Associate General Counsel to the General Conference, brought that issue to my attention. He points out that the denomination's top administrators in September and October 2016 set about to approve a policy for dealing with noncompliant union conferences in spite of the fact that such a policy already existed. According to B 95 15, all such moves in regard to noncompliant unions are to be initiated by the division. And if the division executive committee determines that a union conference/union of churches with conference status is in apostasy or rebellion and should be expelled from the world sisterhood of unions, the division shall refer the matter to the General Conference Executive Committee.[101]

With a clear procedure already in the *Working Policy*, Tyner, with his legal training, wondered out loud why anybody would want to create a new policy. The most likely answer, he points out, "would seem to be that B 95 wasn't exactly what the initiator(s) of this episode wanted to do."[102]

To put it bluntly, the General Conference presidential office had to step outside of policy to make its case for punishing those it deemed to be outside of policy. After all, the *Working Policy* spells out in unmistakable language that dissolution of unions must begin at the division level. But if the division is not likely to come up with the "proper" answer, alternatives must be used. The selected alternative, in this case, was for presidential to step outside of policy to accomplish the task. So *we have a case of blatant noncompliance with the Working Policy to punish noncompliance.*

Obviously, what is needed is a new policy that allows the General Conference president to initiate actions against anybody deemed deserving of such attention. Such a policy, of course, would be a major step toward papalism and unrestricted kingly power.

Tyner points out that General Conference officers "more than once have chosen to ignore policy if it seems the best thing to do, as though policy is optional, not mandatory. *This is a bit like Richard Nixon's position that if the president does it, it isn't illegal.*"[103]

That rather pregnant thought brings us to 2017, during which the Annual Council is to act on the fate of those lower rungs in the organization who are to be dealt with for their own noncompliance on women's ordination. To put it mildly, the leadership of the General Conference has backed itself into an extraordinary situation in the evolution (or revolution) in Adventist authority.

Perhaps at this point in our story we might benefit from a word from the originator of Adventist church structure, who claimed in 1874 that "organization was designed to secure unity of action, and as a protection from imposture. It was never intended as a scourge to compel obedience, but, rather, for the protection of the people of God." Interestingly, James White published that exact statement at least twice, but with different comments each time. In 1874 he added that "church force cannot press the church into one body. This has been tried, and has proved a failure."[104] And in 1880 he added that "those who drew the plan of our church, Conferences, and General Conference organizations, labored to guard the precious flock of God against the influence of those who might, in a greater or less degree, assume the leadership. They were not ignorant of the evils and abuses which had existed in many of the churches of the past, where men had assumed the position which belongs to Jesus Christ, or had accepted it at the hands of their short sighted brethren."[105] And if we need a bit more from his wife, we should recall her statement that the church should think through all the possible consequences of any voted action before legislation is enacted.[106]

With those thoughts in mind we need to remember that the medieval Catholic Church never viewed itself as persecuting anybody. It was just making sure that people were in line with Canon Law, its version of the *Working Policy*.

It has been a long journey, but this chapter must be brought to a conclusion. A little bit of history demonstrates that Adventism's ideas on church authority have come a long way in 150 years. James Standish, formerly of the Religious Liberty department of the General Conference, has written that "as a movement, we are drifting very dangerously into the hierarchicalism, formalism and dogmatism that our pioneers explicitly rejected."[107]

Along that line, we need to remember that part of James White's strategy in getting Adventists to organize in the first place was to help them see that the biblical use of the word "Babylon" not only signified persecution, but also confusion. White sold them on the second meaning. But it appears that the denomination is now intent on resurrecting the first. Of course, given the noncompliance of the General Conference with its own policy, perhaps both meanings are in evidence in 2017.

In the spirit of Luther Year and the General Conference president's call to be faithful to the principles of the Reformation, I am offering my own 9.5 Theses (I do not have time for 95). I want to point out that there are times for soft words. But there comes a time, as Martin Luther discovered, for firm ones. Like Luther, I love my church and hope for its reformation. I believe that Luther wrote his propositions with love in his heart. And I can assure you that I do the same. I really desire to see healing. Here are my 9.5:

9.5 Theses[108]

1. The only basis for Christian unity is Scripture, trust, and the love of God.

2. The *Church Manual* makes it clear that the General Conference is the "highest authority" for the world church, "*under God.*"[109]

3. It is God who calls pastors. All the church can do is to recognize God's call by the laying on of hands.

4. Ordination is not a biblical topic. (The passages using the word in the KJV generally mean to appoint or consecrate.) From the position of the Bible there is absolutely no difference between ordaining and commissioning.

5. For Adventists the Bible is the only source for doctrine and practice. An appeal to policy is not an appeal to the Bible. A vote by a General Conference session is not equivalent to Bible evidence.

6. On issues not definitively settled in the Bible, James White utilized the only possible way forward in unity of mission when he moved from a hermeneutic that stipulated that practices must be expressly spelled out in the Bible to a hermeneutic that held that practices were permissible if they did not contradict Scripture and were in harmony with common sense. (The new hermeneutic made it possible for the Sabbatarian Adventists to organize as a denomination.)[110]

7. The so-called noncompliant unions are not out of harmony with the Bible.

8. Adventism has moved at times from being a church based on Scripture to one based on tradition and ecclesiastical pronouncements.

9. The General Conference leadership in 2017 is coming dangerously close to replicating the medieval church in its call for the serious discipline of large sectors of the church on the basis of a

non-biblical issue.

9.1. The recent General Conference documents and procedures do not reflect faithfulness to the Bible's teachings in Acts 15 or Matthew 18.

9.2. Due to the suppression of data and the manipulation of the events surrounding the voting process, I do not believe that the 2015 vote on women's ordination indicated the voice of God.

9.3. One of the important functions of the ancient Hebrew prophets was to confront priests and kings over their abuse of authority. One of the functions of Ellen White was to confront conference presidents for similar reasons. And, if there were a prophet in modern Adventism, that prophet would find plenty to do.

9.4. The current atmosphere of confrontation in Adventism has not been brought about by the unions, but by the General Conference leadership and its non-biblical and manipulative tactics.

9.45. The October 2017 meetings may help the worldwide Adventist Church decide whether it wants to move more toward an Adventist ecclesiology or toward a more Roman Catholic variety.

9.5 The so-called nonconforming unions must stand together, come into line with General Conference demands, or go down one by one. Martin Niemöller, a leading German Protestant pastor during World War II, has written a thoughtful piece: "First they came for the Socialists, and I did not speak out—because I was not a Socialist. Then they came for the Trade Unionists, and I didn't speak out—because I was not a Trade Unionist. Then they came for the Jews, and I didn't speak out—because I was not a Jew. Then they came for me—and there was no one left to speak out."

In closing, two historical recollections are important. First, Peter's words in Acts 5:29: "We must obey God rather than men" (RSV). Second, Luther's words at the Diet of Worms: "I cannot submit my faith either to the pope or to the councils, because it is clear as the day that they have frequently erred and contradicted each other. Unless therefore I am convinced by the testimony of Scripture...*I cannot and I will not retract*, for it is unsafe for a Christian to speak against his conscience. Here I stand, I can do no other; may God help me. Amen."[111]

Notes

1. "Lebanese University Encouraged to Reach Middle East through Medicine," *Adventist News Network*, May 8, 2017.

2. Heiko A. Oberman, *Luther: Man Between God and the Devil* (New York: Image Books, 1992), p. 204.

3. *Ibid.*, p. 39.

4. Ellen G. White, *The Great Controversy* (Mountain View, CA: Pacific Press Pub. Assn., 1911), p. 126.

5. *Ibid.*, p. 161.

6. *Ibid.*, pp. 204-205.

7. [James White], "The Gifts of the Gospel Church," *Review and Herald,* Apr. 21, 1851, p. 70.

8. Secretariat, General Conference of SDA, "Summary of *A Study of Church Governance and Unity*," Sept. 2016, p. 5; Secretariat, General Conference of SDA, "A Study of Church Governance and Unity," Sept. 2016, p. 13.

9. Ellen G. White, *The Acts of the Apostles* (Mountain View, CA: Pacific Press Pub. Assn., 1911), p. 196; Ellen G. White, *The Story of Redemption* (Washington, DC: Review and Herald Pub. Assn., 1947), pp. 304-306, 308-309.

10. Paul also raises the issue in 1 Cor. 8 and most likely in Rom. 14, but 1 Cor. 10 is the most explicit passage on the topic.

11. Secretariat, "Summary," p. 6, cf. p. 4; Secretariat, "A Study," p. 12.

12. Francis D. Nichol, ed. *The Seventh-day Adventist Bible Commentary* (Washington, DC: Review and Herald Pub. Assn., 1953-1957), vol. 5, p. 448.

13. *Ibid.*, vol. 5, p. 433.

14. Ellen G. White, *Testimonies for the Church* (Mountain View, CA: Pacific Press Pub. Assn., 1948), vol. 7, p. 263.

15. Russell L. Staples, "A Theological Understanding of Ordination," in Nancy Vyhmeister, ed., *Women in Ministry: Biblical and Historical Perspectives* (Berrien Springs, MI: Andrews University Press, 1998), p. 139; see also Darius Jankiewicz, "The Problem of Ordination: Lessons from Early Christian History, " in Graeme J.

Humble and Robert K. McIver, eds., *South Pacific Perspectives on Ordination: Biblical, Theological and Historical Studies in an Adventist Context* (Cooranbong, NSW: Avondale Academic Press, 2015), pp. 101-129.

16. See, e. g., Titus 1:5; Mark 3:14; John 15:16; Acts 1:22; 14:23; 16:4.

17. See Ellen G. White, *Acts of the Apostles*, pp. 161-162.

18. Ellen G. White to Brethren who shall assemble in General Conference, Aug. 5, 1888.

19. Ellen G. White, *Colporteur Ministry* (Mountain View, CA: Pacific Press Pub. Assn., 1953), p. 125. For more on this topic, see George R. Knight, "Visions and the Word: The Authority of Ellen White in Relation to the Authority of Scripture in the Seventh-day Adventist Movement," in Robert L. Millet, ed., *By What Authority? The Vital Question of Religious Authority in Christianity* (Macon, GA: Mercer University Press, 2010), pp. 144-161.

20. For a fuller treatment of the authority crisis in the events surrounding the 1888 General Conference session, see George R. Knight, *Angry Saints* (Nampa, ID: Pacific Press Pub. Assn., 2015), pp. 121-140.

21. G. I. Butler to E. G. White, Oct. 1, 1888; E. G. White to Mary White, Nov. 4, 1888; E. G. White to M. H. Healey, Dec. 9, 1888; cf. E. G. White to G. I. Butler, Oct. 14, 1888.

22. Ellen G. White, "Light in God's Word," MS 37, 1890.

23. Minneapolis *Tribune*, Oct 18, 1888, p. 5; Ellen G. White, "Love, the need of the Church," MS 24, 1892; Minneapolis *Journal*, Oct. 18, 1888, p. 2; italics supplied.

24. Ellen G. White, *Great Controversy*, pp. 289-290; italics supplied.

25. Ellen. G. White, *Acts of the Apostles*, pp. 161-162; italics supplied.

26. Ellen G. White, *Story of Redemption*, p. 304.

27. See *Catechism of the Catholic Church: With Modifications from the Editio Typica* (New York: Image, 1995), pp. 433-437; Jarislav Pelikan, *The Riddle of Roman Catholicism* (Nashville: Abingdon, 1959), pp. 84, 124-125; Richard P. McBrien, *Catholicism*, study edition (San Francisco, Harper & Row, 1981), pp. 558-559, 846-847.

28. The Roman Catholic Church, for example, only has two levels of authority above the local congregation.

29. Joseph Bates and Uriah Smith, "Doings of the Battle Creek Conference, Oct. 5 & 6, 1861," *Review and Herald*, Oct. 8, 1861, p. 148.

30. *Ibid.*

31. George Storrs, "Come Out of Her My People," *The Midnight Cry*, Feb. 15, 1844, pp. 237-238.

32. Charles Fitch, "*Come Out of Her, My People*" (Boston: J. V. Himes, 1843).

33. See George R. Knight, *William Miller and the Rise of Adventism* (Nampa, ID: Pacific Press Pub. Assn., 2010), pp. 228-250.

34. James White, "Yearly Meetings," *Review and Herald*, July 21, 1859, p. 68.

35. *Ibid.*

36. *Ibid.*

37. John Byington and Uriah Smith, "Report of General Conference of Seventh-

day Adventists" *Review and Herald*, May 26, 1863, pp. 204-206.

38. James White, "Organization," *Review and Herald*, Aug. 5, 1873, p. 60.

39. "Sixteenth Annual Session of the General Conference of S. D. Adventists," *Review and Herald*, Oct. 4, 1877, p. 106; italics supplied.

40. Ellen G. White, "Board and Council Meetings," MS 33, [no date] 1891.

41. Ellen G. White to Men Who Occupy Responsible Positions, July 1, 1896.

42. Ellen G. White, "Regarding the Southern Work," MS 37, Apr. 1901.

43. Barry David Oliver, *SDA Organizational Structure: Past, Present and Future* (Berrien Springs, MI: Andrews University Press, 1989), pp. 98-99.

44. Ellen G. White, *Testimonies*, vol. 9, pp. 260-261.

45. For the best treatment on this reorganization, see Oliver, *SDA Organizational Structure.*

46. O. A. Olsen to A. T. Robinson, Oct. 25, 1892; see George R. Knight, *Organizing for Mission and Growth: The Development of Adventist Church Structure* (Hagerstown, MD: Review and Herald Pub. Assn., 2006), pp. 78-80 for the sequence of events.

47. General Conference Committee Minutes, Jan. 25, 1893.

48. *General Conference Bulletin*, May 23, 1913, p. 108.

49. *General Conference Bulletin*, Apr. 3, 1901, p. 26.

50. Ellen G. White, "Regarding Work of General Conference," MS 26, Apr. 3, 1903; italics supplied.

51. Gerry Chudleigh, *Who Runs the Church? Understanding the Unity, Structure and Authority of the Seventh-day Adventist Church* (Lincoln, NE: AdventSource, 2013), p. 18; italics supplied.

52. *Ibid.*

53. Ellen G. White to the General Conference Committee and the Publishing Boards of the Review and Herald and the Pacific Press, Apr. 8, 1894; see also Ellen G. White, *Testimonies*, vol. 9, pp. 259-260.

54. A. G. Daniells, *European Conference Bulletin*, p. 2, cited in Oliver, p. 320.

55. Oliver, pp. 317 n. 2, 341.

56. See Knight, *Organizing*, pp. 133-140.

57. George I. Butler, *Leadership* [Battle Creek, MI: Steam Press, 1873], pp. 1, 8, 11, 13.

58. See, e. g., [James White] in a series entitled "Leadership" that ran in the *Signs of the Times* from June 4, 1874-July 9, 1874; Ellen G. White, *Testimonies*, vol. 3, pp. 492-509.

59. James White and Uriah Smith, "Proceedings of the Fourteenth Annual Session of the S. D. Adventist General Conference," *Review and Herald*, Aug. 26, 1875, p. 59; James White and A. B. Oyen, "Sixteenth Annual Session of the General Conference of S. D. Adventists," *Review and Herald*, Oct. 4, 1877, p. 106.

60. Kevin M. Burton, "Centralized for Protection: George I. Butler and His Philosophy of One-Person Leadership," MA Thesis, Andrews University, 2015.

61. G. I. Butler to E. G. White, Oct. 1, 1888; E. G. White to G. I. Butler, Oct. 14,

1888.

62. See Knight, *Angry Saints*, passim.

63. See Burton, p. 60.

64. Ellen G. White to the General Conference Committee and the Publishing Boards of the Review and Herald and Pacific Press, Apr. 8, 1894; D. T. Jones to J. D. Pegg, Mar. 17, 1890; D. T. Jones to W. C. White, Mar. 18, 1890.

65. Ellen G. White to Elder Daniells and His Fellow Workers, Apr. 12, 1903.

66. Chudleigh, *Who Runs the Church?* p. 31.

67. Stanley E. Patterson, "Kingly Power: Is It Finding a Place in the Adventist Church?" *Adventist Today*, Sept.-Oct. 2012, p. 5; Chudleigh, *Who Runs the Church?* pp. 32-33; *Working Policy of the General Conference of Seventh-day Adventists*, 1999-2000 edition (Hagerstown, MD: Review and Herald Pub. Assn., 2000), pp. 125-126.

68. Rosemary Watts, "North Pacific Reasserts Constitutional Independence," *Spectrum*, Feb. 1987, pp. 29-33. Wilson's letter is found as an appendix on pages 31-33.

69. "Church Leaders Favor Model Constitutions," *Adventist Today*, May-June 1995, p. 19; "Administration Seeks Greater Control," *Adventist Today*, Nov.-Dec. 1994, pp. 23, 26.

70. Susan S. Sickler to George R. Knight, Feb. 27, 2017; Bert Haloviak to George R. Knight, Mar. 7, 2017; "Administration Seeks Greater Control," p. 26.

71. Designated in the *Working Policy* as B 45 in earlier post-1995 editions but now as B 95.

72. Susan S. Sickler to George R. Knight, Feb. 27, 2017; "Administration Seeks Greater Control," pp. 23, 26.

73. Susan S. Sickler to George R. Knight, Feb. 27, 2017; "Administration Seeks Greater Control," pp. 23, 26.

74. See "Administration Seeks Greater Control," p. 26.

75. *Ibid.*, p. 23; Susan S. Sickler to George R. Knight, Feb. 27, 2017.

76. "General Conference Theology of Ordination Study Committee Report, June 2014," pp. 3-7. An examination of the committee membership list reveals that a large portion, if not the majority, were not scholars.

77. Secretariat, "A Study of Church Governance," p. 41; Secretariat, "Summary of *A Study*," p. 14.

78. As will be noted below, many of the TOSC participants were disillusioned when the General Conference president reversed his opinion on the importance of the committee from its first meeting, when it looked as if it would come up with the "proper" answer, to its last, in which the majority voted against his position.

79. TOSC "Report," p. 12.

80. This point needs further investigation into the 13 division reports. Nine divisions in favor of diversity is the lowest number I have come across. Some sources report 11 and others 12 divisions in favor of flexibility.

81. TOSC "Report," pp. 122-123.

82. *Ibid.*, pp. 12, 122-123.

83. Norwegian Union Conference, "A Response to 'A Study of Church Governance and Unity,'" Oct. 4, 2016; See William G. Johnsson, *Where Are We Headed? Adventism after San Antonio* (Westlake Village, CA: Oak and Acorn Publishing, 2017), pp. 153-161 for a published version of the document.

84. Recollections of several participants who wish to remain anonymous.

85. See, e.g., George R. Knight, "The Role of Union Conferences in Relation to Higher Authorities," *Spectrum* (44:4, 2016), p. 40.

86. Secretariat, "Summary of *A Study*," p. 14; Secretariat, "A Study," pp. 40, 41; see also Barry Oliver to George R. Knight, Feb. 20, 2017.

87. Johnsson, *Where Are We Headed?*, p. 1.

88. Ellen G. White to G. I. Butler, Oct. 14, 1888.

89. Secretariat, "A Study," p. 34.

90. Secretariat, "Summary of *A Study*," p. 5; Secretariat, "A Study," p. 13; italics supplied. See also Mark A. Finley, "United in Message, Mission, and Organization," *Ministry,* Apr. 2017, p. 14.

91. Recollections of several participants who wish to remain anonymous.

92. James White, "Leadership," *Signs of the Times,* June 4, 1874, p. 5; italics supplied.

93. Ellen G. White, "Love, the Need of the Church," MS 24, 1892.

94. Ellen G. White, *Special Testimonies: Series A* (Payson, AZ: Leaves-of-Autumn, n.d.), pp. 299-300; italics supplied.

95. Ellen G. White, *Testimonies,* vol. 9, pp. 277-278; italics supplied.

96. See *Working Policy*, L 35, L 50. The sexist language in these sections is not a voted policy, but an editorial decision in the 1980s. See Knight, "The Role of Union Conferences," p. 41; Gary Patterson, untitled critique of the Secretariat's paper on "Unions and Ordination," p. 1.

97. "Session Actions," *Adventist Review*, July 13, 1990, p. 15.

98. See, e.g., Bonnie Dwyer, "General Conference Leadership Considers Takeover of Unions that Ordain Women," Sept. 29, 2016, http://spectrummagazine.org/print/7661.

99. Most of my sources have requested confidentiality, given the intimidating atmosphere in the General Conference building, in General Conference institutions, and among other denominational employees who have hopes for a future in the upper realms of the denomination. In fact, intimidation and threats in matters related to finances and funding have been in the "air" emanating from Silver Spring. It is no accident that no professors from Andrews University or its theological seminary participated in the London Unity 2017 Conference. "Kingly power" is alive and well. It is fortunate that those of us who are retired are beyond that intimidating authority.

100. For one perceptive critique, see Norwegian Union Conference, "A Response to 'A Study of Church Governance and Unity,'" Oct. 4, 2016.

101. Mitchell Tyner, http://spectrummagazine.org/article/2016/10/10/analy-

sis-use-general-conference-working-policy-case-unions-ordain-women.

102. *Ibid.*

103. *Ibid.*; italics supplied.

104. James White, "Leadership," *Signs of the Times*, July 9, 1874, p. 28.

105. James White, "Leadership," *Review and Herald*, June 17, 1880, p. 392.

106. Ellen G. White, *Testimonies*, vol. 9, p. 278.

107. Quoted in Johnsson, *Where Are We Headed?*, p. 74.

108. Even a casual reader will discover that, like Luther, I have had a bit of a challenge keeping the number of theses from expanding—thus the 9.1 and 9.2 maneuver, so that I could maintain the 9.5 symbolism.

109. *Seventh-day Adventist Church Manual*, 16th ed. (Hagerstown, MD: Review and Herald Pub. Assn., 2000), p. 27; italics added.

110. See George R. Knight, "Ecclesiastical Deadlock: James White Solves a Problem that Had No Answer," *Ministry*, July 2014, pp. 9-13; George R. Knight, "James White finds the Answer," in John W. Reeve, ed., *Women and Ordination: Biblical and Historical Studies* (Nampa, ID: Pacific Press Pub. Assn., 2015), pp. 113-120.

111. Ellen G. White, *The Great Controversy*, p. 160.

Part II

Ordination and Hermeneutical Issues

CHAPTER FOUR

The Biblical Meaning of Ordination*

That sounds like a dangerous topic. Certainly a topic that has generated more heat than light, more emotion than knowledge—particularly biblical knowledge. In my 50-some years as an Adventist minister, I have never seen anything that gets people so emotional. So I'm going to try to be unemotional.

Here is my favorite ordination passage: "And when Moses saw that the people had broken loose..." in their experience with the golden calf, "then Moses stood in the gate of the camp, and said, 'Who is on the Lord's side? Come to me.' And all the sons of Levi gathered themselves together to him. And he said to them, 'Thus says the Lord God of Israel, "Put every man his sword on his side, and go to and fro

---

*Chapter 4 is a sermon preached in the Medford, Oregon, Seventh-day Adventist Church on June 20, 2015, just a few days before the beginning of the General Conference session, which would feature a controversial vote on divisions having the option of ordaining women to the pastoral ministry. The sermon was posted on the congregation's website and immediately (and surprisingly) went viral, with tens of thousands of hits on various venues within a few days. The time was right for its message.

That sermon led to an invitation to speak at the Columbia Union's Leadership Summit in March 2016, for which I developed the first two chapters of this book. Those presentations eventuated in an invitation to the Unity Conference in London in June 2017, for which I developed Chapter 3.

The printed sermon found in the present chapter is an edited version of the transcription of the videoed presentation currently found on YouTube and other venues. I have not attempted to make it a polished essay. As a result, it still maintains in many ways an oral style. The sermon may be viewed at https://www.youtube.com/watch?v=GnbkXk6EDFU.

from gate to gate throughout the camp, and slay every man his brother, and every man his companion, and every man his neighbor.'" And the sons of Levi did according to the word of Moses; and there fell of the people that day about three thousand men. And Moses said, 'Today you have ordained yourselves for the service of the Lord'" (Exodus 32:25-29).[1]

That's an interesting ordination passage, isn't it? I've often speculated about using it in an ordination sermon. People kill their wayward neighbors and ordain themselves.

One of the slipperiest words in Scripture is "ordination." The King James Version uses the word "ordain" to translate nearly 30 different Greek and Hebrew words that have a wide range of meaning. And the same can be said for certain other translations. For example, let me go back to the last part of the passage I just read from the Revised Standard Version. Instead of "you have ordained yourselves," the New King James Version says "consecrate yourselves today to the Lord." The New International Version renders it as "you have been set apart to the Lord today" and the New American Standard Bible reads "dedicate yourselves today to the Lord." Most words translated as "ordain" in the King James Version are rendered in modern translations as "set apart," "consecrate," "decided," "chose," "appointed," and so on. Thus while 1 Timothy 2:7 in the King James Version reads, "I am ordained a preacher," all modern translations I examined translate it as I am "appointed a preacher." And whereas the King James Version on Titus 1:5 says "ordain elders in every city," the modern translations I checked say "appoint elders" in every city. The New International Version and many other modern translations do not even use the word "ordain" once in the New Testament.

Before I stood to speak this morning I examined the rather abbreviated concordance in the back of my Revised Standard Version. It has three uses of "ordain" in the New Testament, and none of them have anything to do with ministry. You can go to Bible dictionaries and dictionaries of Greek words and find no entries for the word "ordain." Why? Because ordination is not a biblical topic.

Then where did the word, or use of the word, "ordination" come from? From the history of the early church as it set apart or appointed deacons, elders, and pastors. The word as we use it is never used in Scripture. It's not a biblical topic. Sermon ended!

But not quite! While ordination is not a biblical topic, the Bible does speak of the laying on of hands in setting apart deacons, elders, and pastors. The laying on of hands has a long Old Testament history. It is used, for example, in presenting sacrificial animals. Before certain animal sacrifices, worshippers laid hands on the animal and confessed their sins. In the Old Testament the laying on of hands is used as a blessing, for punishment, for healing, and in Numbers 8:10-11 it is used for a dedication ceremony as the children of Israel put their hands on the Levites to dedicate them to the service of God.

In that last sense, the laying on of hands is picked up in the New Testament. In Acts 6, for example, we find it in connection with the selection of the first deacons in the church. In verses 2-6 we read: "It is not right [Here the apostles are talking. They had been doing a lot of work connected with routine tasks.] that we should give up preaching the word of God to serve tables. Therefore, brethren, pick out from among you seven men of good repute, full of the Spirit [notice they are full of the Spirit before the ceremony] and of wisdom, whom we may appoint to this duty.'... These they set before the apostles, and they prayed and laid their hands upon them." This is the first use of the laying on of hands in the New Testament. It is not referred to as an ordination, but it is a recognition of Spirit-filled individuals who the church chose to publicly recognize and set apart for office by the laying on of hands. However, early in the post-apostolic history of the church the laying on of hands got connected to the word "ordain." Thus the usage is not biblical but post-biblical. And that usage is appropriate if, and only if, we understand the connection between the Bible's use of the laying on of hands and the church's later use of the word "ordination."

But what does the ceremony in Acts 6 mean? Specifically, that the church had verified that certain individuals possessed the Spirit and wisdom and, as a result, decided to set them apart as deacons. And here we should note that nothing was given to them in ordination. The congregation and the leadership of the church recognized that they were already spiritual individuals, then they set them apart. That is the first use of the laying on of hands in the New Testament.

We find something similar in Acts 13. That passage features Paul and Barnabas. The church in Antioch is preparing to send them out on their first missionary tour. "While they were worshiping the Lord and fasting," we read, "the Holy Spirit said, 'Set apart for me Barnabas and Saul for the work to which I have called them.' Then after fasting and praying they laid their hands on them and sent them off" (verses 2-3). Note: before the laying on of hands, they had already been called by God. God called Barnabas and Saul to be the first of what we might call "foreign" missionaries. And before sending them off, the church laid hands upon them. That laying on of hands was not identified as ordination in the Bible. However, it came to be thought of as an ordination as the early church subsequently connected the laying on of hands to the word "ordain."

At this point I am going to read from Ellen White's *Acts of the*

Apostles. Her discussion is helpful. "God foresaw the difficulties that His servants [that is Paul and Barnabas] would be called to meet [when they took the message to the Gentiles], and, in order that their work should be above challenge, He instructed the church by revelation to set them apart publicly to the work of the ministry. Their ordination was a public recognition of their divine appointment to bear to the Gentiles the glad tidings of the gospel.

"Both Paul and Barnabas had already received their commission from God Himself, and the ceremony of the laying on of hands added no new grace or virtual qualification. It was an acknowledged form of designation to an appointed office and a recognition of one's authority in that office. By it the seal of the church was set upon the work of God.... When the ministers of the church of believers in Antioch laid their hands upon Paul and Barnabas, they, by that action, asked God to bestow His blessing upon the chosen apostles in their devotion to the specific work to which they had been appointed.

"At a later date [after Bible times] the rite of ordination by the laying on of hands was greatly abused; unwarrantable importance was attached to the act, as if a power came at once upon those who received such ordination, which immediately qualified them for any and all ministerial work. But in the setting apart of these two apostles, there is no record indicating that any virtue was imparted by the mere act of laying on of hands. There is only the simple record of their ordination and of the bearing that it had on their future work."[2]

The "ordination" or the laying of hands on Paul and Barnabas was a public recognition that God had called and appointed them to be pastoral evangelists, missionary evangelists. Their authority was in the calling, not in the ordination. Ellen White's words are not difficult to understand. But I am going to repeat the basic idea. The laying on of hands transferred no special power or authority. But it was rather a witness to the community that God had called them to a special task. The ceremony was an outward sign that their calling had been acknowledged and recognized by the church. Here is a point that needs to be crystal clear in our minds: Paul and Barnabas, before the laying on of hands, already had the gift of pastoring through the Holy Spirit. Ordination, or the laying on of hands, was only a public recognition of an accomplished fact. Nothing was added through ordination. The church had already seen God's gift in Paul and Barnabas. They had passed the test and the members and leaders were convinced of their calling.

Several other verses, particularly in Timothy and Titus, help us grasp this picture more clearly. 1 Timothy 5:22 tells us that the church should "not be hasty in the laying on of hands." Why? Because the church first needs evidence that individuals have been appointed, that they have been called. 1 Timothy 3:6, in talking about the setting apart of elders or pastors, indicates that an elder or pastor "must not be a recent convert." Why? Because the church needs time to evaluate their spiritual maturity and calling. 1 Timothy 3:10, in talking about the laying on of hands for deacons, notes that people should "be tested first" to evaluate their character. The church is not to lay hands on people who have not been able to demonstrate, to both the leadership and to the congregation, the calling and the appointment of God.

Here we need to summarize the four central points that we have established so far:

1. Ordination itself is not a biblical topic.

2. Laying on of hands is a biblical topic.

3. The church early in its history began to refer to the laying on of

hands as ordination.

4. The ceremony adds nothing to the ordinand. It is rather a public recognition of the gift or calling of a person to God's work.

But what is ordination in the church today? Here the Christian church at large is radically divided between two forms of ordination that have little in common. On one hand, we find the general Protestant view, which is that ordination is an outward act of recognition of God's gift rather than a channel of power. On the other hand, the Roman Catholic alternative is that ordination provides power and authority not possessed before. Probably the best way to arrive at a better understanding of the two views of ordination is to look at the varying understandings of baptism and the Lord's Supper.

The Bible teaches that baptism is an outward witness to the community of an inward dedication to God. First individuals dedicate their life to God, and then they undergo baptism as a public witness to the community of that decision. Thus baptism is an outward symbol of an inward change. That is the biblical view. What began to happen in the history of the church is quite different. The Roman Catholic view is that baptism cancels the effects of original sin, removes guilt, and forgives all sin. From that perspective, there is power in baptism. It takes away, even for a baby, the penalty of original sin—kind of like magic. It is not an outward sign but a major transaction with saving aspects in itself.

Next, we need to look at the Lord's Supper. The general Protestant view is that it is a memorial of what Jesus did on the cross 2,000 years ago. The Bible says that we are to partake of the symbols as a remembrance that Christ died for our sins on the cross once for all. But in the Roman Catholic Mass it is not a memorial service but a sacrifice repeatedly performed by a priest. According to the Council of Trent, it is a true sacrifice in which the priest has the power to change the bread into the actual flesh of Christ. That is power! Meanwhile, the wine is transformed into the actual blood of Christ. The Mass atones for the sin of those who partake of it. Thus it is a salvational event. The priest has power. And where did the priest get that mighty power? Through the ordination service. According to Catholic teaching, ordination confers on a man the power of consecrating and offering the body and blood of Christ and of forgiving or remitting sin.[3] Thus for Roman Catholics ordination entails an immense transfer of power and authority. But please remember that that understanding is a post-biblical perspective. Most Protestants view ordination as an outward act indicating public recognition of a person's call to ministry.

So what is pastoral ordination? If it is recognition that a person has been called to pastoral ministry, we must understand the nature of ministry before the question can be answered intelligently. Probably the best biblical definition of ministry is found in 2 Timothy 4:2-5, a passage often used in ordination services. "Preach the word, be urgent in season and out of season, convince, rebuke, and exhort, be unfailing in patience and in teaching.... Always be steady, endure suffering, do the work of an evangelist, fulfill your ministry." Presenting the topic from another angle, I have often told my students that the heart of ministry is to love God's people and to preach God's Word. From the biblical perspective, a person who is successfully performing the work of ministry is eligible to be set apart by the laying on of hands.

But here we need to ask a crucial question: How does a person become a pastor or minister? Ephesians 4:8, 11-12 tells us that when Jesus ascended He provided spiritual gifts for the church. "His gifts were that some should be apostles, some prophets, some evangelists, some pastors and teachers, to equip the saints for the work of ministry, for building up the body of Christ." Please note that the gifts in Ephesians are not gender oriented. Nowhere does the list say "males only." After all, the Bible does have female prophets. It has female preachers for that matter. Who decides who receives which gift? On that point the Bible is clear. It is not me or you or the church that decides who gets the various gifts. The Bible tells us that the Holy Spirit distributes the gifts (1 Corinthians 12:4, 7, 11, 28), rather than some earthly church. The Holy Spirit both calls and equips a person for ministry. The church, in ordination or the laying on of hands, merely recognizes in a public way what the Holy Spirit has already done.

So why am I even talking about this topic today? I'll tell you one reason. Pastor Randy received five books on the topic of ordination in the mail this week, and he didn't order any of them. And those five are merely the tip of an iceberg. Ordination currently is a hot topic in Adventism. My wife and I leave for San Antonio, Texas, next week, where the General Conference of the Seventh-day Adventist Church will be meeting in its quinquennial session. And one of the most controversial issues of the session is a vote related to the ordination of female pastors by those world divisions who desire to do so. There is a good reason why our pastor asked me to talk on this subject today. Namely, that the ordination of women is a topic that many feel could split the Adventist church. And it could if we operate on heat and emotion rather light and biblical understanding. Thus we had better be very clear on what the Bible says regarding ordination. The issue is not one of ministry for women. I'm going to say that again in case some people have wax in their ears, or, like me, are just plain hard of hearing. The issue is not one of ministry for women. That has already been decided. God used women all the way through Scripture. Try

Deborah for a woman who had authority over men. And Joel 2:28 tells us that we are yet to see young women having prophetic visions at the end of time. Then there are such female leaders in the New Testament as the four daughters of Philip, Priscilla, Phoebe the deacon,[4] Junia, who Paul in Romans 16:7 calls an apostle,[5] and others. Women have always had a place in the ministry of both Testaments. And the Adventist church has approved officially the roles of female pastors and local elders. Beyond that, it formally ordains female elders and commissions female pastors, both through the laying on of hands.

However, it is a man's world. Thus females have had an uphill battle. Up until recent times women were often thought of as possessions. But my wife does not consider herself to be a possession. If I took that approach it would be the end of me! Times have changed. In the time of Christ a Jewish male thanked God in prayer every morning that he was not a Gentile, not a slave, and not a woman. Even in the United States women did not have the right to vote until 1920. And a married woman in the early 19th century could not in many states own her own property. It belonged to her husband, even if she brought it into the marriage. All down through history men have run the show. And maintaining male power has been a crucial aspect of history. But such passages as Galatians 3 signaled a new course when Paul wrote that "as many of you as were baptized into Christ have put on Christ. There is neither Jew nor Greek, there is neither slave nor free, there is neither male nor female; for you are all one in Christ Jesus" (verses 27-28).

The church has had a difficult time with all three parts of that response to the Jewish prayer. Just think of the struggle to get Gentiles into the church on an equal basis with Jews. The Jews attempted to keep them out unless they first became Jewish. Then there was the issue of slavery, with part of the church using selected Bible passages to justify keeping people in servitude. The United States finally settled that issue by a deadly Civil War in the 1860s. But the most persistent of all discriminations has been the sexual. Women have faced discrimination down through history, including in the "enlightened" Christian West.

Even our Bible translations have succumbed to that discrimination. One example is found in Romans 16:1, which speaks of Phoebe the "deaconess" (e.g., RSV). That is very interesting since the Bible knows of no order of deaconesses. In the Greek, Phoebe is called a *diakonos*, meaning deacon. And deacons were set apart by the laying on of hands in the New Testament. But large sectors of the post-biblical church have created the order of deaconess, and have traditionally not set them apart by the laying on of hands. Adventism in the past followed that less-than-biblical path. A second example of verbal discrimination is located in Romans 16:7, where we find Andronicus and Junia labeled as "apostles." Some translations have added the word "men" after those two names (see e.g., RSV), even though the gender description is not found in the Greek New Testament and Junia was undoubtedly a female.[6] We need to recognize that Bible translators have generally been men; men who have often brought their own prejudices to their task.

And male prejudices are not limited to Bible translators. I have been surprised by some of the arguments my seminary students have used against the ordination of women. One of the more interesting ones, put forth by one of my African students in the late 1980s, was that there were no female priests in the Old Testament. Several others jumped in with agreement. Good point, they argued.

And he did have a point. There were indeed no female priests in the Old Testament. I let them hash that obvious point over a bit and then noted that there were no black priests in the Old Testament either. I was quick to add that the same was true of European whites. All the priests were of Asian decent. But not just Asian, but of Hebrew lineage, but even then all were from the tribe of Levi of the family of Abraham. In fact, they were all sons of Aaron. I suggested to my students that they needed to be careful about how they tried to prove a point.

But they were not finished yet. The next argument raised used the passage in Timothy that says that an elder must be "the husband of one wife" (1 Timothy 3:2). Here was the clincher. They now had a Bible verse to prove their point. After all, from the biblical perspective, only males could have a wife. Slam dunk; problem solved!

Maybe. But that interpretation does have some problems. After all, it has the slight disadvantage of locking both Jesus and Paul out of the ministry. Think about it. Jesus, not having a wife, wouldn't qualify. And Paul was in the same boat. Watch out how quick you draw your gospel gun and start blazing off into the night. Every Bible passage has a context. And the "one wife" passage was super appropriate in the Greco-Roman world, where it was not a social problem to have a lady on the side, or a little boy for that matter. What Paul is telling us in First Timothy is that pastors could not have more than one wife; they could have one and only one. They needed to be moral, which meant no concubines, polygamy, or other relationships on the side.

But, some of my students remonstrated, a woman isn't supposed to speak in public; they are to "learn in silence" and keep quiet (1 Timothy 2:11-12). Once again, Paul is dealing with a local problem in Greek culture in which it would have been inappropriate for women to have a public role. But the Bible has females speaking out publicly in both Testaments. And the silence-only rule, if followed consistently, would put nearly all Adventist congregations in a tight spot. I've seen several women up front in church today speaking and leading the song service. That is hardly being silent in church. Beyond that, this particular congregation has three female elders. In Greek culture females did not have that freedom. And Paul had to fit into that Greek world.

All down through history, including in the New Testament, we find God using women in public religious roles. That is not the issue. The problem we are facing today is the ordination of women as ministers. But is that a real problem? Only if one has a Roman Catholic view of ordination. I am going to say that again. Ordination of females is only a problem if one has a Roman Catholic view of ordination, in which a priest is called "Father" and ordination adds almost magical, and even god-like, power. But if nothing is added except public recognition of what has already taken place in a person's calling and ministry, then ordination is not as crucial an issue as some Adventists would like to make it. It is merely recognizing what is already taking place. And here we have an interesting situation in that many female pastors are doing a much better job in pastoral ministry than many of their male counterparts.

But if no mysterious or spiritual power is added at ordination, then the ordination of women is a non-issue, even though some see it as the ultimate heresy. Such individuals fail to understand the biblical meaning of ordination. Interestingly, in Seventh-day Adventism both male and female pastors have their ministry recognized by the laying on of hands. By General Conference action female pastors possess all the rights and prerogatives of male pastors, except that they cannot be ordained and therefore cannot serve as conference presidents.

Let me be clear here, pastors of both sexes in Adventism receive recognition by the laying on of hands. But for men it is called "ordination," while for women it is called "commissioning." Do you understand what I just said? They all do the same thing, they all have the same ministry, they all have the same laying on of hands, yet they are certified by different words. And in that the church is merely playing a word game. For men, the exalted group, we call it "ordination." For women we call it "commissioning." But from a biblical perspective they are exactly the same thing.

In December 2012 I held a seminar for the division leadership of the church in the United States and Canada and suggested that since ordination is not a biblical word, we should just drop the word; get rid of it. Of course, that would do away with a lot of medieval history. I told them I was willing to turn in my ordination papers and they could give me a card stating that I was a commissioned minister. Big deal. It doesn't make any real difference. Just solve the problem, get rid of the troublesome, non-biblical word. But getting rid of the word for those who see something magical in it, or powerful in it, is heresy. So, like I said earlier, the whole topic of ordination is high on heat and low on light; high on emotion but weak on biblical knowledge.

I like Ellen White's approach to the topic. She held that her ordination came from God. While she held a certificate of ordination from the General Conference, she had never been ordained by a man. She didn't need it. She had been called and ordained (appointed) by God.

I took the same position in my own ministry. Having a rather unique situation, I was not ordained until I was 55—almost ready to die! I remember receiving phone calls from conference presidents asking if I would preach ordination sermons. My standard reply was that I would preach the sermon as long as they did not ask me to lay hands on anybody. That statement was followed by silence at the other end of the line. Finally, the inevitable "Why not?" would come through. "Because I am not ordained." No problem. I went and preached the ordination sermon anyway. I never worried about ordination or even holding ministerial credentials. For more than a decade I was the only professor in the Seventh-day Adventist Theological Seminary who did not hold so much as a ministerial license. But I preached all over the place to the people and dignitaries of the church, including for the General Conference. I never had a concern about ordination because I knew that it was merely an outward recognition of the call of God. And I had the call from God, so I was not concerned with the recognition of humans.

But when I was 54 I received a phone call asking me if I would like to be formally ordained. I replied that it didn't matter to me, but if they really had a burden to ordain me they could call the next year and ask again. So they phoned when I was 55 and asked again. And I said yes, if you really want to ordain me, we can move forward with that recognition.

But, I need to ask, what happened when I was ordained? What happened in my ministry? NOTHING DIFFERENT! I continued to do what I had been doing for years. I did feel good that they gave me a little piece of paper. But that was it. God had appointed me (ordained me) as a minister, and if God calls a person, human ordination is only a recognition of that fact. But if a person does not have the call of God, ordination means nothing. We need to get it straight on the biblical meaning of ordination.

As we go through these next few months, we need to keep our

church and its members in our prayers on this topic. No matter which way the vote goes in San Antonio, there are going to be a lot of disappointed people. My prayer is that somehow we might begin to grasp more clearly what the Bible really teaches about ordination and the laying on of hands and what has made the topic so divisive in the history of the church. We need to realize that it is the church history aspect, particularly the medieval definitions that, as Ellen White put it, gave ordination "unwarrantable importance,"[7] that has made it an explosive topic today.

And here I must be frank: I can understand why Roman Catholics might be upset by the ordination of women; and I can perhaps even understand why Baptists might have a problem; but I'm having a really difficult time with Adventists. Let's face it: the most influential clergy person in the history of Adventism has been a female—Ellen White. And she spoke out loud in churches all over the place and she had spiritual authority over men. For Adventists to be struggling over the ordination of women in ministry is simply incomprehensible to me. But if I were the devil, I'd push everybody's buttons except their biblically-thinking button. My only conclusion is that there are a whole lot of confused Adventists out there. Let's pray.

Notes

1. Unless otherwise indicated, all Scripture quotations are from the Revised Standard Version of the Bible.

2. Ellen G. White, *The Acts of the Apostles* (Mountain View, CA, 1911), pp. 161-162; italics supplied.

3. See Jaroslav Pelikan, *The Riddle of Roman Catholicism: Its History, Its Beliefs, Its Future* (Nashville, TN: Abingdon Press, 1959), pp. 110-127.

4. The Greek in Romans 16:1 says "deacon." The New Testament knows of no order of deaconess. Both males and females were deacons.

5. See Nancy Vyhmeister, "Junia the Apostle," *Ministry*, July 2013, pp. 6-9.
6. Ibid.
7. Ellen G. White, *Acts of the Apostles*, p. 162.

CHAPTER FIVE

Proving More Than Intended*

Surprising as it may seem, we sometimes prove more than we set out to if we extend our methodology to its logical conclusions.

The Case of Jewelry

For example, some have argued that one of the best reasons for modern Christians to not wear jewelry is that we are currently living in the antitypical day of atonement.

In the Old Testament the annual Day of Atonement was the most solemn day in the Jewish calendar. It was a day of self-examination, judgment, and cleansing. And it wasn't just a day for the priests to offer special sacrifices. Every individual had to be involved, lest he or she be "cut off." Repeatedly the Israelites were told to "afflict" themselves on that most solemn day (see Leviticus 16:29-30; 23:27, 32; Numbers 29:7, RSV). "Whoever is not afflicted on this same day shall be cut off from his people" (Leviticus 23:29). It was a serious day indeed.

---

*This chapter was written in response to a presentation opposed to the request of the North American Division at the 1995 General Conference session for each division to have the option of ordaining female pastors. I was dumbfounded by the logic used by the presenter and the argument's hermeneutical implications. It was first published by *Ministry* in March 1996. The only revisions have been technical, but I have provided several endnote references that were missing earlier.

"The commandment to 'afflict yourselves,'" writes Gordon Wenham, "underlined the need for every individual to examine himself and repent of his sins."[1] Others have argued that part of this affliction would be humility and plainness of dress. Thus those truly searching their hearts would put aside their jewelry.

I find this to be an interesting position. But it seems to me that it is simpler to prove that one shouldn't have sex on the antitypical day of atonement. After all, Leviticus 15:16-18 says that those who have sexual intercourse are ceremonially unclean until evening. That implies that they would be disqualified from performing the religious duties of the annual Day of Atonement. When that interpretation is extended to the antitypical day of atonement, it becomes even more fascinating. It is one thing to not have sex on a holy day; it is quite another to not participate in it during the entire time of the antitypical period. Of course, those with a proclivity toward such an application can also find eschatological justification for their position. After all, doesn't Revelation 14:1-5 teach that the 144,000 will be "virgins"? While some may jump for joy over such an interpretation, others would probably see it as more "affliction" than they are happy to deal with.

Of course, it is even more easily proved by the above line of logic that all work is forbidden in the antitypical day of atonement (Leviticus 23:28, 30, 31; Numbers 29:7). But while that point is most easily proved, the average mind doesn't find its consequences nearly so interesting to contemplate as the no-sex argument.

At this juncture it is important for me to point out plainly that I am not arguing either for or against jewelry, sex, or work. My point has to do with the proper use of Scripture. Specifically, I am pointing out that we sometimes inadvertently prove more than we intend through our use of logic as it relates to the Bible. It is important also to note that I do not doubt the sincerity of those who have set forth such arguments. The issue is one of methodology rather than sincerity. There may be excellent arguments against the use of jewelry (and sex and work) in the Bible, but it seems to me that the argument related to the antitypical day of atonement is not one of them. Typology (as is also true of parables), while valid for many inferences, has definite limitations.

The Case of the Ordination of Women

Another illustration of an argument that proves more than intended has to do with the ordination of women. The Seventh-day Adventist Church (along with several other denominations) has seen a great deal of argumentation on both sides of the topic for the past few years.

One speaker recently based his argument against women's ordination on the fact that the Adventist Church is a church of the Bible and thus "God's Word must be our focus."[2] Given that solid foundation, he quite appropriately quoted Isaiah 8:20: "To the law and to the testimony: if they speak not according to this word, it is because there is no light in them" (KJV).

He next guided his hearers to the "timeless message" of 1 Timothy 2, emphasizing especially verse 12: "I do not permit a woman to have authority over a man."[3] That was followed by a threefold argument favoring male leadership.

This speaker was quite certain that Paul's advice had nothing to do with culture. To the contrary, the counsel was set forth as a universal moral imperative, and transgressing it means nothing less than "the derailment of a mission-driven church."[4]

The real issue, he asserted, was that we trust the Bible writers. At that point the argument became even more intense and certainly more interesting from a hermeneutical perspective. "Now the question is," he said to his audience, "How do we interpret the Bible?" His reply was that the Bible doesn't need interpretation. Or, as he put it: "The Word of God is infallible; accept it as it reads. We have plenty of counsel about the danger of modifying God's instructions.... What we need as Seventh-day Adventists, friends, is submission to the Word of God, not reinterpretation."[5]

Subsequently, he cited Ellen White as saying that "the Lord will have a people upon the earth to maintain the Bible and the Bible only as the standard of doctrine and the basis of all reform." He concluded his study in part by claiming that he was against the ordination of women to ministry because "it violates the doctrine of the Holy Scriptures by not accepting Scripture as it plainly reads."[6]

What Was Really Proved?

There is no doubt that he was speaking the honest convictions of his heart. Yet I sat dumbfounded as I read and contemplated his forceful presentation. For one thing, 1 Timothy 2:12 says absolutely nothing about ordination. Then again, I could hardly believe the presentation came from a Seventh-day Adventist—maybe a conservative Calvinist, but not an Adventist. After all, Adventists have the phenomenon of Ellen White. I was struck full in the face with the fact that, if one accepted his presuppositions, what had actually been demonstrated was that Ellen White is a false prophet.

Roger Coon illustrates my point well when he relates his experience with an itinerant evangelist who came to Napa, California, and placed a large advertisement in the local newspaper promising to destroy the doctrines of the Seventh-day Adventist Church in a presentation on Thursday evening and demolish their prophet the following week. Coon attended both sessions. In the second, the evangelist "proved" the Seventh-day Adventist Church was a false church because one of its primary founders was a woman who defied the teachings of the apostle Paul forbidding women to speak in Christian churches.

Adventists, for obvious reasons, have always resisted that interpretation. The church has traditionally justified Ellen White's public ministry by noting that the counsel given about women being silent in church in 1 Timothy 2:11-12 was rooted in the custom of time and place and was not to be woodenly applied now that conditions had changed. Thus, as *The Seventh-day Adventist Bible Commentary* puts it: "Because of the general lack of private and public rights then accorded women, Paul felt it to be expedient to give this counsel to the church. Any severe breach of accepted social custom brings reproach upon the church.... In the days of Paul, custom required that women be very much in the background."[7]

Let's return to our Adventist speaker and examine a bit more carefully his use of 1 Timothy 2. The first thing to note is that he read only that portion of the passage that suited his purpose. The words immediately preceding the partial verse he quoted were: "A woman should learn in quietness and full submission" (1 Timothy 2:11, NIV). And the words immediately following the "timeless message" he read merely reinforce that sentiment. His paraphrase also left out the words "to teach or" since his only focus was on the restriction dealing with "authority." Let me quote verse 12 in full: "I do not permit a woman to teach or to have authority over a man; she must be silent" (NIV).

Now it is obvious that if one is testing everything in the strictest sense by the words of the law and the testimony, and if one is not "modifying" God's instructions (or interpreting them), but simply accepting Scripture as it "plainly reads," then it is a necessary conclusion that Ellen G. White must be a false prophet of the most serious type.

To put it mildly, she seldom remained silent in church. In fact, she taught authoritatively to men and women everywhere she went. She was the ultimate transgressor if in fact 1 Timothy 2:11-12 is expressing a "timeless message" that doesn't need interpretation.

Let's face it: after one examines all the arguments on headship and/or the significance of Eve's sinning before Adam—and after one is exposed to all the fine points of argument coming from the biblical Greek and Hebrew and the scholarly German and French—the plain fact is that the Bible says in unmistakable English that women are not to teach and that they are to be silent.

Of course, if one's hermeneutic allows for the consideration of the time and place in which Scripture was written, then the problem isn't nearly as serious. But our friend allowed himself no such out. Thus he is stuck with the fact that when tested by a "plain reading" of the Bible, Ellen White is a false prophet. He had proved more than he intended.

On the other hand, if one concedes that the part about silence needs to be "modified" a bit (should I be bold enough to say "interpreted" or "contextualized" to time and place?), then one must also grant that such license must be extended to the whole verse. But that, of course, would lead to an undermining of the entire argument. While that might seem frightful to some, the only alternative is to be stuck with a false prophet.

The fine points of my argument seem to have been missed by two recently published books that follow the same general line of argument as discussed above. Both see 1 Timothy 2:11-14, along with the somewhat parallel passage in 1 Corinthians 14:34-35, as being crucial texts in the case against ordination (even though neither passage mentions the topic), both see the issue as being one of biblical authority, and both take the position that the Bible can be faithfully read only as it is.

Having said that, however, they immediately begin to modify and interpret the part about women being silent in church. As one of the volumes points out, "the issue here is not muzzling women into silence."[8] The other book claims that the 1 Corinthians passage "certainly does not really mean" that women have to be silent in church, since that "would contradict other Pauline teaching." "The conclusion is that the restriction" on women speaking in church "must be in reference to authoritative teaching that is a part of the pastoral office, the position of leadership and spiritual authority over a congregation."[9]

Now, that is an interesting interpretation, but it doesn't get Ellen White off the false prophet hook. After all she spoke quite authoritatively, even to the leading ministers both in the church and out. In fact, she found herself often enough in public conflict with male ministers, and she managed to argue quite authoritatively in spite of Paul's injunction.

It is an interesting point that for some years Ellen White held ministerial credentials and her credentials were those of an ordained minister, even though she was never technically ordained by the laying on of human hands. She was (and is) the most "authoritative" minister the Seventh-day Adventist Church has ever had. If anyone in Adventism—male or female—has ever spoken with authority, it has been Ellen White.

When the second of these recently published books comes to explaining the significance of the statement about women being silent in 1 Timothy 2:11-14, it arrives at the apex of modification and adapted interpretation. "What is prohibited to women," our author tells us, "is teaching in the worship services as a part of the ecclesiastical office of pastor, which involves the exercise of spiritual authority. Women who are asked to participate in worship services, whether by praying or exhorting, do so on the basis of the authority delegated by the male pastor who holds the ecclesiastical office and whose spiritual authority is derived from Christ."[10]

So much for not interpreting and for reading just the plain words of the Bible.

Even that massive reconstruction of the text doesn't get Ellen White off the hook. She exercised spiritual authority in public and in private, and her hearers were both male and female. Of course, people can continue to finesse their definitions so as to make Paul come out with their conclusions, but doing that is hardly a reading of the "plain words" of the Bible. And such a procedure most certainly fails to follow its own hermeneutical method to its logical conclusions.

Some Final Thoughts

Before moving away from the stimulating topic of women's ordination, perhaps I should share one more argument that proves more than intended. One day in my pastoral formation class one of my students came up with the "airtight answer" to the issue of women's ordination. "Read the Old Testament," said he. "Every ordained priest was a male."

"True," I replied, "but you have proved too much if you stick to your argument. If you follow your logic, you will have to conclude that very few, including you, are biblically eligible for ordination, because the Old Testament approved only the ordination of male Orientals. And even at that, not just any Oriental would do. They had to be Hebrew, and then only of the Aaronic line of the Levitical family."

"Well," say some who want to extend the argument, "look at Jesus. He appointed only male disciples." True, but it can just as truly be argued that He appointed only non-Diaspora Jewish disciples. Let's be faithful to the logic of our own arguments.

"But," says another, "Paul was a male from the Diaspora who was 'kind of' a disciple, even though not one of the twelve." Yes, but some of the original non-Diaspora male disciples might point out that Paul is where all the trouble began. After all, look at the problems he raised when he began to apply the gospel to the context of first-century Gentiles. He nearly split the New Testament church. "But," yet another suggests, "that's why Paul's experience is in the Bible. With him all justifiable contextualization must cease. After all, you can't go to extremes on this business of applying the Bible to new times and places."

The arguments can go on and on. And they will.

In closing I want to say again that the topic of this chapter is not jewelry, sex, work, or the ordination of women. Rather, it is a caution to examine the full consequences of our theological method lest we prove more than we intend; it is a plea to be faithful to our own logic and to the totality of the texts selected to demonstrate our point. Thus jewelry and ordination merely provide contemporary illustrations that prompt a call for the sound use of Scripture. After all, there is a major difference between using the Bible to prove a point and developing a sound biblical argument. A "high view" of the Bible demands a wholesome hermeneutic.

Notes

1. Gordon J. Wenham, *The Book of Leviticus, The New International Commentary on the Old Testament*, (Grand Rapids, MI: William B. Eerdmans Pub. Co., 1979), p. 237.

2. P. Gerard Damsteegt, presentation at "Thirteenth Business Meeting, Fifty-sixth General Conference session, July 5, 1995, 2:00 p.m.," *Adventist Review*, July 7, 1995, p. 25.

3. Ibid., p. 26. The Bible quotation is a paraphrase.

4. Ibid.

5. Ibid.; italics supplied.

6. Ibid.; italics supplied. The quotation comes from Ellen G. White, *The Great Controversy* (Mountain View, CA: Pacific Press Pub. Assn., 1911), p. 595. Damsteegt in typical oral style modified the exact wording but faithfully presented its essence.

7. Francis D. Nichol, ed., *The Seventh-day Adventist Bible Commentary* (Washington, D.C.: Review and Herald Pub. Assn., 1953-1957), vol. 7, pp. 295-296.

8. Samuel Koranteng-Pipim, *Searching the Scriptures: Women's Ordination and the Call to Biblical Fidelity* (Berrien Springs, MI: Adventists Affirm, 1995), p. 58.

9. C. Raymond Holmes, *The Tip of an Iceberg: Biblical Authority, Biblical Interpretation, and the Ordination of Women in Ministry* (Berrien Springs, MI: Adventists Affirm and POINTER Publications, 1994), p. 142; italics in original.

10. Ibid., pp. 144-146; italics in original.

CHAPTER SIX

Ecclesiastical Deadlock: James White Solves a Problem That Had No Answer*

C hurch organization was one of the hardest fought battles in Adventism's early years. Extending over nearly two decades, the struggle not only eventuated in aspects of church order not even suggested in Scripture, but provided a key hermeneutical principle for deciding other topics not made explicit in the Bible.

In the process, James White and many others experienced a

---

*Chapter 6 was originally written for *Women and Ordination: Biblical and Historical Studies*, which was published by Pacific Press in April 2015. Edited by John W. Reeve, the book was initiated by a special committee of the Seventh-day Adventist Theological Seminary. The book's aim was to help educate the denomination on issues related to the ordination of women as the church moved toward its 2015 General Conference session.

The title of this chapter in that book was "James White Finds the Answer." A shortened version was published under the current title in *Ministry* in July 2014. It focused on the hermeneutical key that allowed early Adventists to make decisions on topics not adequately covered in Scripture. The purpose of the publication of the material in *Ministry* was to set forth a model of how the Adventist pioneers worked through issues not settled in Scripture that might aid the members of the Theology of Ordination Study Committee. Unfortunately, the Committee had completed its task by the time the article had worked its way through the publication process.

NOTE: This chapter has been drastically abbreviated in order to cut out much of the needlessly redundant material that is also found in Chapter 1. Some redundancy remains. But that which remains presents a focused argument that is not only historically important but is also crucial to finding a breakthrough to current issues troubling the denomination.

hermeneutical metamorphosis—a necessary transformation that allowed Seventh-day Adventism to develop into the worldwide force that it is today. Without the change, Adventism would probably still be a backwater religious group largely confined to the Northeastern and Midwestern United States.

Deadlock

George Storrs set forth the basic position for the Adventist struggle over organization in 1844 when he proclaimed that "no church can be organized by man's invention but what it becomes Babylon *the moment it is organized.*"[1] That proclamation rang true to a generation of Adventists who had been persecuted by their denominations as Millerism reached its crest in 1843 and 1844.

Of course, some of the founders of what became Seventh-day Adventism didn't need much help on the anti-organizational front. For James White and Joseph Bates the stance came naturally since they had come from the Christian Connexion, which had no effective church structure above the congregational level.[2] Even Ellen White, who came from the highly structured Methodist Episcopal Church, had seen the Babylonianish characteristics of her denomination as it defrocked ministers for advocating Millerism, sought to silence members who wouldn't be quiet on the topic, and disfellowshipped those who chose not to obey that hierarchical order—including her own family who faced a church trial and lost their church membership in 1843.[3]

It is no accident that the earliest Sabbatarian Adventists were suspicious of the persecuting power of Babylon. They had felt the power of church structures in a way that wasn't pleasurable or, they believed, even Christian.

But as the Sabbatarians began to develop their own congregations in the early 1850s, they soon realized that symbolic Babylon had more than one meaning in the Bible. It could represent not only a persecuting entity but also confusion. It is that latter definition that James and Ellen White began to emphasize by late 1853 as they faced the problems of a disorganized movement that had little sense of direction and no structure above the congregational level.[4]

Even Bates was on board regarding the need for church order of some sort. In harmony with his Connexionist background, Bates claimed that biblical church order must be restored to the church before the Second Advent. He argued that during the Middle Ages the "law-breakers" "*deranged*" such essential elements of Christianity as the Sabbath and biblical church order. God had used the Sabbatarian Adventists to restore the seventh-day Sabbath and it was "perfectly clear" to his mind "that God will employ law-keepers as instruments to restore...a 'glorious Church,' not having spot or wrinkle.... This unity of the faith, and perfect church order, never has existed since the days of the apostles."[5]

By 1853 the problem wasn't seeing the need for church structure; rather, it was biblical justification for such a move. And that need takes us to early Adventist hermeneutics.

Hermeneutical Transformation and the Way Forward

While Bates was quite certain that the apostolic order of the church needed to be restored, he made no room for any element of organization not found explicitly in the New Testament. James White at this early period shared a similar opinion. Thus he could write in 1854 that "by gospel, or church order we mean that order in church association and discipline taught in the gospel of Jesus Christ by the writers of the New Testament."[6] A few months later he spoke of the "perfect system of order, set forth in the New Testament by inspiration of God.... The Scriptures present a perfect system, which, if carried out, will save the Church from imposters" and provide the ministers with an adequate platform for carrying out the work of the church.[7] J. B. Frisbie, the most active writer in the *Review* in the mid-1850s on church order, agreed with Bates and White that every aspect of church order needed to be *explicitly spelled out in the Bible.*[8]

With their literalistic biblical approach to church order, it is of little surprise that Frisbie and others soon began to discuss the ordination of deacons, local elders, and pastors. By the mid-1850s they were ordaining all three classes.[9]

Gradually they were strengthening gospel order at the level of the local church. In fact, the individual congregation was the only level of organization that most Sabbatarians gave much thought to. Thus such leaders as Bates could preface an extended article on "Church Order" with the following definition: "Church, signifies a particular congregation of believers in Christ, united together in the order of the gospel."[10]

But in the second half of the 1850s the church-order debate among Sabbatarians would focus on what it meant for congregations to be "united together." At least five issues would force leaders such as James White to look at church organization more globally. The first had to do with the legal ownership of property—especially the publishing office and church buildings. Other issues included the problems of paying preachers, the assignment of preachers to work locations, the transfer of membership between congregations, and the question of how independent congregations should relate to each other. The problems related to the paying and assigning of preachers were especially difficult since the Sabbatarians had no settled pastors. The issues the young movement faced logically led to thinking beyond the congregational level.

By 1859 those concerns were joined by others, including the need to extend missionary labor to new fields. Those needs and others drove James White to progressively urge the need for a more complex and adequate form of church structure.

"We lack system," he cried out in the *Review* on July 21, 1859. White let it be known that he was sick and tired of the cry of Babylon every time that anyone mentioned organization. "We venture to say that there is not another people under heaven more worthy of the brand of Babylon than those professing the Advent faith who reject Bible order. Is it not high time that we as a people heartily embrace everything that is good and right in the churches? Is it not blind folly to start back at the idea of system, found everywhere in the Bible, simply because it is observed in the fallen churches?"[11] White firmly believed that in order to get the Advent movement moving it had to organize. That task he would pursue with full vigor between 1860 and 1863.

Meanwhile, James's strategic place in the Sabbatarian movement had given him a scope of vision that not only separated him from the reasoning processes of many of his fellow believers, but had transformed his own thinking. Three points White raised in 1859 are of special importance as we look forward to his organizing activities in the early 1860s.

First, he had moved beyond the biblical literalism of his earlier days when he believed that the Bible must explicitly spell out each aspect of church organization. In 1859 he argued that "we should not be afraid of that system which is not opposed by the Bible, and is approved by sound sense."[12] Thus he had come to a new hermeneutic. *He had moved from a principle of Bible interpretation that held that the only things Scripture allowed were those things it explicitly approved to a hermeneutic that approved of anything that did not contradict the Bible and good sense.* That shift was essential to the creative steps in church organization he would advocate in the 1860s.

That revised hermeneutic, however, put White in opposition to those, such as Frisbie and R. F. Cottrell, who continued to maintain a literalistic approach to the Bible that demanded that it explicitly spell something out before the church could accept it. To answer that mentality, White noted that nowhere in the Bible did it say that Christians should have a weekly paper, operate a steam printing press, build places of worship, or publish books. He went on to argue that the "living church of God" needed to move forward with prayer and common sense.[13]

White's second point involved a redefinition of Babylon, noting that it not only signified persecution but also confusion. His third point concerned mission. Sabbatarians must organize if they were to fulfill their responsibility to preach the three angels' messages.

Thus between 1856 and 1859 White shifted from a literalistic perspective to one much more pragmatic. A second round in the hermeneutical struggle took place when James White raised the question of incorporating church property in February 1860 so that it could be legally held and insured. He bluntly stated that he refused to sign notes of responsibility for individuals who desired to lend their money to the publishing house. Thus the movement needed to make arrangements to hold church property in a "proper manner."[14]

White's suggestion called forth a vigorous reaction from R. F. Cottrell (a corresponding editor of the *Review* and the leader of those opposed to church organization) in March 1860. On April 26 James White published an extensive reply to Cottrell in which he raised again the hermeneutical argument that he had used against the biblical literalists in 1859. Acknowledging that he could find no plain text of Scripture for holding property legally, he pointed out that the church did many things for which it could find no Bible text. He then moved on to Jesus' command to let "your light so shine before men," pointing out that He did "not give all the particulars how this shall be done." At that point he wrote that *"we believe it safe to be governed by the following RULE. All means which, according to sound judgment, will advance the cause of truth, and are not forbidden by plain scripture declarations, should be employed."*[15] With that declaration White placed himself fully on the platform of a pragmatic, common sense approach to all issues not definitely settled in the Bible. Ellen White supported her husband in his struggle with Cottrell.[16]

The hermeneutical struggle renewed in October 1860 as the property difficulty came to a head at a conference James White called in Battle Creek to discuss the problem along with the related issues of legal incorporation and a formal name, a requirement for incorporation. Between September 29 and October 2, 1860, delegates from at least five states discussed the situation and possible solutions in great detail. All agreed that whatever they did should be according to the Bible, but, as we might expect, they disagreed over the hermeneutical issue of whether something needed to be explicitly mentioned in the Bible. James White, as usual, argued that "every Christian duty is not given in the Scriptures."[17] That essential point had to be recognized before they could make any progress toward legal organization. Gradually, as the various problems and options surfaced, the majority of the candidates accepted White's hermeneutical rule.

The October 1860 conference accomplished several main goals. The first involved the adoption of a constitution for the legal incorporation of the publishing association. The second was that "individual churches so...organize as to hold their church property or church buildings legally." James White, still fighting the hermeneutical battle with the proof-texters, twice called the objectors to produce "one text of scripture to show that this is wrong." Not being able to find such a passage or to match his logic, the objectors surrendered and the motion carried.[18]

Concluding Thoughts

The above discussion appears to be one concerned with issues related to church organization. But that is only a surface reading of what took place. Undergirding each round of the struggle was something much more basic and important—the hermeneutical issue.

The early 1850s found all of the Sabbatarians in a literalistic, proof-texting frame of mind. Without an explicit text on a topic they would not and could not move forward.

James White found his way out of the rigid cul-du-sac in which they were trapped by revising his hermeneutics. He had come to realize that "we should not be afraid of that system which is not opposed to the Bible, and is approved by sound sense."[19]

With that hermeneutical breakthrough he provided the means by which he and his wife could guide the young movement into a mission to all the world. Without it, Seventh-day Adventism would have been hampered in its mission, as was every other branch of the Millerite movement. All, except the Sabbatarians, remained small and ineffective. All remained trapped in an inflexible hermeneutic that failed to let them operate effectively in the real world of doing church.

And what does James' new hermeneutic have to do with the topic of women in ministry, or even the ordination of women? EVERY-THING!

A Postscript for Those Who Don't Get the Point

Several concerns directly relate to James White finding the hermeneutical key to issues not conclusively settled in the Bible, particularly those related to women in ministry and the ordination of women. The first is that there is no biblical text or texts on either side of the discussion that conclusively settle the issue of ordination. If there were, the debate would be over.

Of course, some put forward the male headship argument as the conclusive answer. But that is a disastrous approach for those who take the Bible seriously. After all, the Bible is clear that Christ is the only head of the Christian church and that all Christians are brothers and sisters in the body of that church (Ephesians 1:22-23; 4:15-16; Colossians 1:18). The Bible puts forth no intermediary position between Christ as head and believers as the body. Male headship theology may be at the heart of Roman Catholic ecclesiology, but it has never been so in Adventism, which has traditionally advocated the New Testament's teaching on the priesthood of all believers (1 Peter 2:9). The Bible's teaching regarding male headship is framed in terms of family relationships rather than ecclesiastical (Ephesians 5:22-25; 1 Corinthians 11:3).[20]

Another attempt to find a biblical answer to issues related to the ordination of females is to appeal to such texts as 1 Timothy 2:11-15 and 1 Corinthians 14:34-35 as the final answer. However, such an appeal not only has its own exegetical issues but is very problematic for Seventh-day Adventists. I demonstrate in another connection that such argumentation merely proves that Ellen White is a false prophet. After all, she spoke publicly all over the place and most certainly had "authority over men."[21]

The natural fallback argument to that logic is that Ellen White was a prophet rather than a pastor. But that response contains the seeds of its own destruction in that it violates the plain words of Scripture, which says "woman" rather than "every woman except a female prophet." Here we must ask the question of just how much violence against the Bible is allowed in our attempt to defend a certain, preferred reading of a text.

Given Ellen White's prominence in Adventism, passages such as 1 Timothy 2:11-12 and 1 Corinthians 14:34-35 had to be addressed early on and continuously in the denomination's history. Up until the time when the ordination of women issue arose, the Adventist response had been consistent. Namely, that the counsel given about women was rooted in the custom of time and place and was not to be woodenly applied in a world in which conditions had changed. Thus, as *The Seventh-day Adventist Bible Commentary* puts it: "Because of the general lack of private and public rights then accorded women, Paul felt it to be expedient to give this counsel to the church. Any severe breach of accepted social custom brings reproach upon the church.... In the days of Paul, custom required that women be very much in the background."[22] The Adventist unanimity on the cultural interpretation of the passages, of course, hit a brick wall when the agenda of supporting the validity of Ellen White's ministry ran head-on into the agenda of keeping women "in their place." As might be expected, the new agenda of some has led to some interesting exegetical exercises that would have been strange fire indeed to James White, J. N. Andrews, J. H. Waggoner, and the other early Adventists, who consistently supported the cultural understanding of the disputed passages.[23]

Notes

1. George Storrs, "Come Out of Her My People," *The Midnight Cry*, Feb. 15, 1844, p. 238.

2. See George R. Knight, *Organizing to Beat the Devil: The Development of Adventist Church Structure* (Hagerstown, MD: Review and Herald Pub. Assn., 2001), pp. 15-18.

3. Arthur L. White, *Ellen G. White: The Early Years, 1827-1862* (Washington, DC: Review and Herald Pub. Assn., 1985), pp. 43-44.

4. [James White], "Gospel Order," *Review and Herald*, Dec. 6, 1853, p. 173; Ellen G. White, *Early Writings* (Washington, DC: Review and Herald Pub. Assn., 1945), p. 97.

5. Joseph Bates, "Church Order," *Review and Herald*, Aug. 29, 1854, pp. 22-23.

6. [James White], "Gospel Order," *Review and Herald*, Mar. 28, 1854, p. 76.

7. [James White], "Church Order," *Review and Herald*, Jan. 23, 1855, p. 164.

8. J. B. Frisbie, "Church Order," *Review and Herald*, Dec. 26, 1854, p. 147.

9. See George R. Knight, "Early Seventh-day Adventists and Ordination, 1844-1863." In Nancy Vyhmeister, *Women in Ministry: Biblical and Historical Perspectives* (Berrien Springs, MI: Andrews University Press, 1998), pp. 101-114.

10. Joseph Bates, "Church Order," *Review and Herald*, Aug. 29, 1854, p. 22.

11. James White, "Yearly Meetings," *Review and Herald*, July 21, 1859, p. 68.

12. *Ibid.*

13. *Ibid.*

14. James White, "Borrowed Money," *Review and Herald*, Feb. 23, 1860, p. 108.

15. James White, "'Making Us a Name,'" *Review and Herald*, Apr. 26, 1860, pp. 180-182, italics supplied.

16. Ellen G. White, *Testimonies for the Church* (Mountain View, CA: Pacific Press Pub. Assn., 1948), vol. 1, p. 211.

17. James White, in "Business Proceedings of B. C. Conference," *Review and Herald*, Oct. 16, 1860, p. 169.

18. *Ibid.*, pp. 170-171.

19. James White, "Yearly Meetings," *Review and Herald*, July 21, 1859, p. 68.

20. See "On the Headship of Christ in the Church: A Statement of the Seventh-day Adventist Theological Seminary, Andrews University," in John W. Reeve, ed., *Women and Ordination: Biblical and Historical Studies* (Nampa, ID: Pacific Press Pub. Assn., 2015), pp. 39-45.

21. See Chapter 5.

22. Francis D. Nichol, ed., *The Seventh-day Adventist Bible Commentary*, (Washington, DC: Review and Herald Pub. Assn., 1957), vol. 7, pp. 295-296.

23. Denis Fortin, "What Did Early Adventist Pioneers Think About Women in Ministry," Apr. 8, 2010, http://www.memorymeaningfaith.org/blog/2010/04/adventist-pioneers-women-ministry.html.See also, Theodore N. Levterov, "The Development of the Seventh-day Adventist Understanding of Ellen G. White's Prophetic Gift, 1844-1889" (Ph.D. dissertation, Andrews University, 2011), passim.

Made in the USA
San Bernardino, CA
11 November 2017